D1487729

Checklist for Life
for Graduates

Presented To:

_____

Presented By:

_____

Date:

_____

Checklist for Life
for Graduates

Checklist for Life
for Graduates

NELSON BOOKS
A Division of Thomas Nelson Publishers
Since 1798

www.thomasnelson.com

Published in Nashville, Tennessee, by Thomas Nelson, Inc.

Managing Editor: Lila Empson
Manuscript written by Marcia Ford
Design: Whisner Design Group

Library of Congress Cataloging-in-Publication Data

Checklist for life for graduates.
    p. cm.
    ISBN 0-7852-6186-9 (pbk.)
    1. Youth--Religious life. 2. Youth--Conduct of life. I. Thomas Nelson Publishers.
    BV4531.3.C475 2004
    248.8'34--dc22

    2004001456

Heart Attitude

I am confident that God has His hand on my life.

Table of Contents

Table of Contents Continued

Introduction

Oh, taste and see that the LORD is good; blessed is the man who trusts in Him!

PSALM 34:8 NKJV

Have you ever been so excited in your life? Here you are, a graduate—ready to take on the world. No one can hold you back now. You're pumped, you're primed, you're prepared. It's time to get on with real life.

If that's *not* the way you're feeling right now, you're not alone. Your peers may seem as if they're ready to roll, but it's likely that deep down, they're feeling at least some measure of uncertainty. Those who have decided to continue on with their education may be wondering if they have chosen the right school for their field of study. Friends entering military service have their own set of concerns, from the stories they've heard about basic training to the places of unrest to which they may be sent. Those going into the workplace may be questioning if they can cut it in a clearly adult environment.

What you could use right now is a guidebook, a manual for survival in the world you're about to enter. You probably already have the most important one—the Bible. In its pages you'll find the wisdom you need to navigate your way through adulthood. Consider the book you're holding to be a companion to your Bible, a handbook designed to assist you in those first critical years after you've graduated and left home.

Look over the table of contents and the first few chapters to get an idea of how this manual is organized. Use the book however you like, either reading each chapter in sequence or turning to a topic of particular interest to you on any given day. The important thing is to use it. As you check off each item that you accomplish, you can gain a greater sense of achievement and progress on the path to adulthood.

Keep your Bible and a notebook nearby as you work your way through the book. It's time to get going—on a truly exciting adventure, now that you know you have the tools you need.

Maturity begins to grow when you can sense your concern for others outweighing your concern for yourself.
—JOHN MACNAUGHTON

Watch, stand fast in the faith, be brave, be strong.

1 CORINTHIANS 16:13 NKJV

Work will win when wishy-washy wishing won't.

THOMAS S. MONSON

[Jesus said,] "Take My yoke upon you and learn from Me, for I am gentle and lowly in heart, and you will find rest for your souls."

MATTHEW 11:29 NKJV

God wishes to test you like gold in the furnace. The dross is consumed by the fire, but the pure gold remains and its value increases.

JEROME EMILIANI

Beloved, building yourselves up on your most holy faith, praying in the Holy Spirit, keep yourselves in the love of God, waiting anxiously for the mercy of our Lord Jesus Christ to eternal life.

JUDE 20–21 NASB

It is not your business to succeed, but to do right; when you have done so, the rest lies with God.

C. S. LEWIS

To insure good health: Eat lightly, breathe deeply, live moderately, cultivate cheerfulness, and maintain an interest in life.
WILLIAM LONDEN

Checklist for Life *for Graduates*

Facing it, always facing it, that's the way to get through.
Face it.
> —Joseph Conrad

You will show me the path of life; in Your presence is
fullness of joy; at Your right hand are pleasures
forevermore.
> —Psalm 16:11 NKJV

I Will

Be aware of the danger signs around me.

yes ___ *no* ___

Respond immediately to the warning signals of God's Spirit.

yes ___ *no* ___

Look out for the physical and spiritual safety of others.

yes ___ *no* ___

Realize that my adversary, the devil, is out to bring me down.

yes ___ *no* ___

Acknowledge my increased level of vulnerability.

yes ___ *no* ___

Depend on God for the strength to walk away from potentially dangerous situations.

yes ___ *no* ___

Learn to enjoy life even as I remain watchful.

yes ___ *no* ___

Things to Do

☐ *Read Jesus' parables in Matthew 24 and 25 to see how He illustrated the concept of watchfulness.*

☐ *List those areas of your life in which you know you are particularly vulnerable.*

☐ *Ask God to always protect you and keep you alert when your vulnerabilities are exposed to danger.*

☐ *Find a spiritual "lifeguard buddy," a friend with whom you share the responsibility to be on guard for each other.*

☐ *Read Mark 13:35-37 for an illustration of the need for round-the-clock vigilance.*

Things to Remember

The end of all things is at hand; therefore be serious and watchful in your prayers.

1 PETER 4:7 NKJV

Be watchful in all things, endure afflictions, do the work of an evangelist, fulfill your ministry.

2 TIMOTHY 4:5 NKJV

Watch, stand fast in the faith, be brave, be strong.

1 CORINTHIANS 16:13 NKJV

[Jesus said,] "If he comes suddenly, do not let him find you sleeping. What I say to you, I say to everyone: 'Watch!' "

MARK 13:36–37 NIV

[Jesus said,] "Watch and pray, lest you enter into temptation. The spirit indeed is willing, but the flesh is weak."

MARK 14:38 NKJV

God's people avoid evil ways, and they protect themselves by watching where they go.

PROVERBS 16:17 CEV

Every man who observes vigilantly and resolves steadfastly grows unconsciously into genius.

EDWARD G. BULWER-LYTTON

They that are on their guard and appear ready to receive their adversaries are in much less danger of being attacked than the supine, secure, and negligent.

BENJAMIN FRANKLIN

I Will

Pay attention to the wisdom of the "Jethros" in
my life.

yes *no*

Ask God to help me manage my life.

yes *no*

Realize that doing too much can make me ineffective.

yes *no*

Acknowledge that even an important activity must
be held in check.

yes *no*

Understand that spiritual failure in any area will
affect all the other areas of my life.

yes *no*

Appreciate the great variety in the life God has
given me.

yes *no*

Things to Do

☐ *Read a book on organizing your life, such as Bobb Biehl's* On My Own
Handbook.

☐ *Ask God to show you where your life may be out of balance.*

☐ *Ask God to show you which areas of your life need more attention right
now.*

☐ *Write down on an index card what God shows you and tape it to your
mirror.*

☐ *Read the story of Jethro and Moses in Exodus 18.*

☐ *Assess the health of your body, your mind, and your spirit; do
something today to make each one healthier.*

Things to Remember

"Martha, Martha," the Lord answered. "You are worried and upset about many things. But only one thing is needed. Mary has chosen what is better. And it will not be taken away from her."

LUKE 10:41-42 NIrV

[Jesus said,] "Take care to live in me, and let me live in you. For a branch can't produce fruit when severed from the vine. Nor can you be fruitful apart from me."

JOHN 15:4 TLB

[Jesus said,] "The thorny ground represents those who hear and accept the Good News, but all too quickly the message is crowded out by the cares of this life and the lure of wealth, so no crop is produced."

MATTHEW 13:22 NLT

In all matters requiring wisdom and balanced judgment, the king found the advice of these young men to be ten times better than that of all the magicians and enchanters in his entire kingdom.

DANIEL 1:20 NLT

Just as your car runs more smoothly and requires less energy to go faster and farther when the wheels are in perfect alignment, you perform better when your thoughts, feelings, emotions, goals, and values are in balance.

BRIAN TRACY

The foundation stones for a balanced success are honesty, character, integrity, faith, love and loyalty.

ZIG ZIGLAR

Single-Mindedness

Sharp Focus

Set your mind on things above, not on things on the earth.

After a grueling three and a half years of college, Justin was finally able to relax. He had planned his course schedule so that during the final semester before graduation he would have to take only twelve credits, leaving him plenty of time for a part-time job and a volunteer position with a campus ministry.

Then the manager of the mall store where he had worked throughout his college years made him a tantalizing offer: He could become an assistant manager, with a significant pay raise and a guaranteed forty-hour workweek with benefits. If he accepted the position, Justin could easily afford the payments on a shiny new car he'd had his eye on for the last few weeks, plus meet his living expenses and have money left over for some fun now and then.

This was too good to be true. He thought it over, made an appointment to meet with his manager, and was all set to accept the offer. "Of course, this means you'll have to work until closing every weeknight and all day on Sunday," his manager said. "You'll have to cover for the other employees if we're shorthanded." Justin's heart sank. He faced a dilemma: Give up his position with the ministry and miss church every Sunday, or give up the notion of having that shiny new car and money to spare.

It didn't take long for Justin to decide. During a training session for volunteer workers the previous month, the director of the campus ministry had given a teaching on Matthew 6:19-34, stressing the impossibility of serving two masters. That teaching hit home and hit hard in this situation. Thanking his manager for placing so much faith in his abilities, he declined the offer and elected to keep his part-time job. Though he still wanted the car as much as ever, he felt an immediate sense of peace and relief, knowing the choice he made was the right one.

Jesus made the observation that a person who tries to serve two masters will end up hating one master and loving the other. Justin knew his choice wasn't really between working full time and working part time. It came down to serving God or serving money; he knew he couldn't have it both ways. He chose God, the only master worth serving and worth loving. He remained focused on the things above, not on the things of earth.

In the context of faith, that's what single-mindedness is all about. It means making the Lord the top priority in your life, the center around which everything else in your life revolves. That doesn't mean you need to spend every waking moment thinking about God, though please feel free to do so. It means that you view every aspect of your life from the perspective of your relationship with Him.

You are constantly faced with dilemmas that pit one master against another. Your boyfriend wants to take your relationship to a more intimate physical level. Your roommate wants you to give Buddhism a chance. Some of your friends want you to go clubbing over the weekend . . . every weekend. There are moments when you want to do one or two things that aren't on any list of wholesome activities that you're aware of.

But no. If you have made the decision to live in a Christ-centered way, then ultimately you have set your mind on things above. Your loyalty, your allegiance, is to Jesus alone. To do anything that would grieve Him or run contrary to God's will is out of the question. The course you have chosen for your life has made you single-minded. You want what God wants for you and nothing less.

The Lord in His graciousness has given you freedom of choice. You are the only one who can decide what your priorities will be. Will you continue to place God and the things of the Spirit first, or will the lure of the world and material things divert your attention from the things above? If you have set a single-minded course for your life, then you already know the answer, because your heart is set on God and on Him alone.

I Will

Keep my mind and heart set on the things above.   yes ___   no ___

Learn to see every aspect of my life from the
perspective of my relationship with God.   yes ___   no ___

Be thankful for the freedom of choice God has
given me.   yes ___   no ___

Remember that God is the center around which
everything else in my life revolves.   yes ___   no ___

Trust God to help me when I am tempted to serve
two masters.   yes ___   no ___

Strive to please God in all that I do.   yes ___   no ___

Things to Do

☐ *Read Matthew 6:19-34 and think about the entire passage from the perspective of choosing to serve one master.*

☐ *Meditate on what it means to make God the number one priority in your life.*

☐ *Make a list of those areas in your life right now in which you are tempted to serve two masters. Make a conscious decision for God in each area.*

☐ *Memorize two of the Bible verses on the following page.*

☐ *Enlist a friend's help in keeping you focused on God and pledge to do the same for him.*

☐ *Look at your activities during a typical week and eliminate anything that conflicts with your single-minded loyalty to God.*

Things to Remember

The people said to Joshua, "We will serve the LORD our God. We will obey him alone."

JOSHUA 24:24 NLT

Jesus answered, "I am the way and the truth and the life. No one comes to the Father except through me."

JOHN 14:6 NIV

[For] the doubter, being double-minded and unstable in every way, must not expect to receive anything from the Lord.

James 1:7 NRSV

There is only one God and one Mediator who can reconcile God and people. He is the man Christ Jesus.

1 TIMOTHY 2:5 NLT

I will lie down and sleep in peace, for you alone, O LORD, make me dwell in safety.

PSALM 4:8 NIV

Draw near to God and He will draw near to you. Cleanse your hands, you sinners; and purify your hearts, you double-minded.

JAMES 4:8 NASB

Do not fear anything except the LORD Almighty. He alone is the Holy One. If you fear him, you need fear nothing else.

ISAIAH 8:13 NLT

Simon Peter replied, "Lord, to whom would we go? You alone have the words that give eternal life."

JOHN 6:68 NLT

Worship and glory belong forever to the eternal king, the immortal, invisible, and only God. Amen.

1 TIMOTHY 1:17 GOD'S WORD

There is only one Lord, one faith, one baptism, and there is only one God and Father, who is over us all and in us all and living through us all.

EPHESIANS 4:5–6 NLT

O LORD, you alone can heal me; you alone can save. My praises are for you alone!

JEREMIAH 17:14 NLT

It seems essential, in relationships and all tasks, that we concentrate only on what is most significant and important.

SÖREN KIERKEGAARD

Singleness of purpose is one of the chief essentials for success in life, no matter what may be one's aim.

JOHN D. ROCKEFELLER

Biblical Worldview

An Intelligent Defense

See to it that no one takes you captive through hollow and deceptive philosophy, which depends on human tradition and the basic principles of this world rather than on Christ.

COLOSSIANS 2:8 NIV

Now that you are graduated and on your own, you need to make sure you are well-grounded in your understanding of what you believe and why. Your new freedom will bring about new experiences, many of which will challenge your beliefs. How will you respond when you are confronted with ideas that run counter to what you believe to be true?

Most of the people who hold unbiblical views are not out to intentionally erode the foundations of the Christian faith. The problem is that their worldview is shaped by principles and beliefs that cannot be found anywhere in the Bible. It's critical that you understand that, just as it's critical for you to develop a rock-solid biblical worldview. What does that mean? It means that everything you believe about God and ultimate truth and humankind and your purpose here on earth can be supported by principles found in the Bible.

Take, for example, the value you place on human life. If you genuinely believe in the biblical principle that life is sacred and every person is precious in the eyes of God, your worldview will differ drastically from that of someone who believes all life is a result of chance. As a consequence, you can expect that such things as your attitude toward the elderly and the unborn and your political stance will differ as well. Contradictory views and arguments may sound reasonable, but you will not be swayed because your belief is grounded in the truth of the Bible.

If you are not sure what you believe, the time has come to make sure. Examine the claims of Christ and the Bible. Get clear on the larger biblical concepts: God's plan of redemption through the work of Jesus Christ, His activity and intervention in human history, and the ongoing ministry of His Spirit. You are an intelligent being, and God expects you to use your mind as well as your spirit in developing your faith. You can examine Christianity on an intellectual level without any fear of losing your faith, because Christianity and the Bible are both intellectually defensible.

The Bible can withstand your scrutiny, and one of the most important side effects of that scrutiny is that you'll come away with a rock-solid biblical worldview. You'll become acutely aware of the deception and falsehood apparent in other worldviews—all but guaranteeing your immunity to those deceptive viewpoints.

I Will

Understand that everyone has a worldview, whether or not they can define it.

yes _____ _no_ _____

Realize that everything I do, every decision I make, stems from my worldview.

yes _____ _no_ _____

Nurture my faith intellectually.

yes _____ _no_ _____

Discover for myself that Christianity is a rationally defensible faith.

yes _____ _no_ _____

Be ready to give a defense of my faith to anyone who asks.

yes _____ _no_ _____

Be aware of other worldviews evident throughout society.

yes _____ _no_ _____

Things to Do

☐ _Read_ A Ready Defense _or another book by Josh McDowell, whose skepticism as a college student turned into a solid biblical worldview._

☐ _This week, spend time studying one major biblical concept, such as God's plan of redemption._

☐ _Read a column or other opinion piece in a newsmagazine such as_ Time _or_ Newsweek _and see if you detect any evidence of a Christian worldview._

☐ _Write out a clear defense of your faith—why you believe what you believe._

☐ _Find a group of believers with whom you can openly discuss the questions you have about your faith._

Things to Remember

Sanctify Christ as Lord in your hearts, always being ready to make a defense to everyone who asks you to give an account for the hope that is in you, yet with gentleness and reverence.

1 PETER 3:15 NASB

While Paul was waiting for [Silas and Timothy] in Athens, he was deeply troubled by all the idols he saw everywhere in the city. He went to the synagogue to debate with the Jews and the God-fearing Gentiles, and he spoke daily in the public square to all who happened to be there.

ACTS 17:16–17 NLT

God has overlooked the times when people did not know him, but now he commands all of them everywhere to turn away from their evil ways.

ACTS 17:30 GNT

How then shall they call on Him in whom they have not believed? And how shall they believe in Him of whom they have not heard? And how shall they hear without a preacher?

ROMANS 10:14 NKJV

A conversion is incomplete if it does not leave one with an intense social consciousness, if it does not fill one with a sense of overwhelming responsibility for the world.

WILLIAM BARCLAY

[The Bible] is an interpretation of human history as a whole, beginning with the saga of creation and ending with a vision of the gathering together of all the nations and the consummation of God's purpose for mankind. The Bible is an outline of world history.

LESSLIE NEWBIGIN

Brokenness

Grief Transformed

The LORD is near to those who have a broken heart, and saves such as have a contrite spirit.

PSALM 34:18 NKJV

Perhaps you heard about Reg and Maggie Green, an American couple whose young son was shot and killed by bandits as they traveled through Italy late one night. The story was a gripping one: a child, sleeping peacefully in the backseat, ruthlessly gunned down by criminals who misidentified the car. So compelling was this story that it was later filmed as a made-for-TV movie, *Nicholas's Gift.*

This was not a story to the Greens; this was their son's life. What they chose to do to honor his life transformed their sorrow into an act of love and forgiveness: They decided to donate their son's organs to prolong and improve the lives of others. Italians were overwhelmed by their kindness; support for organ donation soared throughout Italy, where the practice had been frowned on. In the years since, thousands of lives have been saved thanks to one couple who allowed their grief to be transformed.

By the time most people reach their late teens and

early twenties, they've suffered some kind of loss in their lives. Maybe a close relative or a close friend of yours died—or maybe a love relationship died. You probably already know what it's like to feel broken, shattered, or splintered. It's hard, very hard, to come to terms with some of the events in life that threaten to undo you. You may wonder at times how you'll ever get through it without completely crumbling. You have an edge: You know where to turn for the relief you need from the grief you feel.

The crushing weight of circumstances that break your heart serves an immediate and eternal purpose: It sends you straight to God for comfort, and God is always near, His arms outstretched to draw you close to Him where He can hold you and console you and give you hope in the midst of the darkness around you.

You will not always understand the bad things that happen to you and those you love. But you can be assured that the temporary pain and heartache you experience in this life will be transformed into eternal glory in the next life. Never forget that you cannot place your hope in this world. Keep trusting in God and placing your hope in Him, the One who promises to heal your broken heart and fill your life with joy and peace.

I Will

Remember where to go when circumstances
threaten to undo me.

yes _____   _no_ _____

Allow God to comfort and console me when I
experience personal loss.

yes _____   _no_ _____

Understand that nothing has ever broken that
God could not repair.

yes _____   _no_ _____

Always expect some good to come from painful
experiences.

yes _____   _no_ _____

Be willing and prepared to console others when
they suffer loss.

yes _____   _no_ _____

See both the immediate and eternal purposes in
the losses I suffer.

yes _____   _no_ _____

Things to Do

☐ _Read the story of the prodigal son in Luke 15, noting how the
son's brokenness drove him to his father's arms._

☐ _Consciously forgive anyone who has caused you to grieve, no
matter how recent or long ago it's been._

☐ _Read about Joni Eareckson Tada, who allowed God to transform
her brokenness into a ministry that reaches millions of people._

☐ _Pray Psalm 34 back to God._

☐ _Read any of the Gospel accounts of Christ's suffering on the cross
to get a glimpse of how He was broken on your behalf._

☐ _Meditate on what it means to have God's Spirit as your Comforter._

Things to Remember

He heals the brokenhearted and binds up their wounds.

PSALM 147:3 NKJV

May the God of hope fill you with all joy and peace as you trust in him, so that you may overflow with hope by the power of the Holy Spirit.

ROMANS 15:13 NIV

This is my comfort in my affliction, for Your word has given me life.

PSALM 119:50 NKJV

Young women will dance and be glad. And so will the men, young and old alike. I will turn their sobbing into gladness. I will comfort them. And I will give them joy instead of sorrow.

JEREMIAH 31:13 NIrV

I will set out and go back to my father and say to him: Father, I have sinned against heaven and against you. I am no longer worthy to be called your son; make me like one of your hired men.

LUKE 15:18–19 NIV

Men . . . are bettered and improved by trial, and refined out of broken hopes and blighted expectations.

FREDERICK W. ROBERTSON

The world breaks everyone and afterward many are stronger at the broken places.

ERNEST HEMINGWAY

Wisdom

A Generous Gift

The fear of the LORD is the beginning of wisdom; a good understanding have all those who do His commandments. His praise endures forever.

PSALM 111:10 NKJV

What comes to your mind when you think of someone giving you a generous gift? More than likely, you think of something that's valuable—maybe even priceless. Did you know that God has promised to give you something in this life that is both valuable and priceless? It's the gift of wisdom, and it's yours for the asking.

Most of the wisdom you acquire will come over the course of a lifetime, but you can ask God to begin giving you wisdom now. Unlike knowledge, the facts and information you have been learning over the years in school and elsewhere, wisdom is a constantly growing accumulation of insights into how to live, how to make the right decisions, and how to best put to use all that knowledge you have gained. The good news is that you don't have to wait until you're older to be considered a wise person; you can begin to acquire wisdom no matter how young you are.

Your next step should be to search the Bible for evidence of God's wisdom. You can do this in a direct way, by using an online Scripture search site to find every verse in the Bible that uses words like *wisdom* and *wise*, or you can do this simply by being attentive to the underlying principles and truths that relate to wisdom in your regular Bible reading. Better yet, use both methods.

Now you are ready to start putting what you have learned about wisdom to good use in your everyday life. You do that by training yourself to see connections between what God shows you through His Word and what you experience throughout the day. Here's an example: One morning in your devotions you read Proverbs 15:31: "The ear that hears the rebukes of life will abide among the wise" (NKJV). Later that day, your boss tries to show a coworker—for the third time—a better way to pack the merchandise that needs to be shipped out. Your coworker thinks his way is better, and he begins to develop a bad attitude.

What is the connection? What can this incident teach you about acquiring wisdom? Look at your coworker's attitude. His ears did not hear the rebuke your boss wanted him to hear. Will he "abide among the wise"? It's not likely, is it? A person who pays attention to a rebuke and learns from it displays a humble, teachable spirit; a person who does not exhibits a prideful, closed spirit. Without a teachable spirit your coworker has little hope of acquiring wisdom. That insight can serve as a lesson to you.

Keep your spirit open to the wisdom that comes from

God. You may find it exhibited in any number of places: in the example of others, in the teachings you hear from the pulpit, in the Christian books you read, and even in the Christian songs you listen to. Allow His wisdom to settle into your spirit.

Give yourself a head start on wisdom by using your youth to your advantage; learn to recognize the wisdom that comes from God, and learn to incorporate its lessons into your life now, while you are still young.

As you stand poised on the brink of a new chapter in your life, you could do yourself a favor by placing wisdom high on your list of priorities. The earlier you begin to look at life from the perspective of wisdom, the greater your potential for living a productive and fulfilling life that is pleasing to God. Not just any wisdom—the world has its own brand of wisdom, and that's not the kind you will profit from—but the wisdom that comes from God, the wisdom found throughout the Bible. His wisdom not only has withstood the test of time but also will continue throughout eternity, after this world and its best ideas are long gone.

You can begin by asking God to open your eyes and ears to the wisdom that comes from Him. The Bible promises in James 1:5 that He will "generously" grant you wisdom. Now that's getting off to a pretty good start.

Teach me true wisdom.
—PSALM 51:6 CEV

I Will

Place wisdom high on my priority list. _____ *yes* _____ *no*

Recognize the difference between God's wisdom and the world's wisdom. _____ *yes* _____ *no*

Discover what the Bible says about wisdom. _____ *yes* _____ *no*

Count on God to give me a greater measure of wisdom. _____ *yes* _____ *no*

Learn to make connections between what I read in the Bible and what I experience in life. _____ *yes* _____ *no*

Realize that I don't have to wait until I am old to become wise. _____ *yes* _____ *no*

Things to Do

☐ *Ask God to generously give you His wisdom.*

☐ *Using an online searchable Bible, such as one found at www.crosswalk.com, look up verses that relate to wisdom.*

☐ *Start a "Wisdom" page in your journal to which you will add wisdom verses as they appear in your regular Bible reading.*

☐ *Memorize Proverbs 3:13-15, which describes wisdom as worth more than gems or precious metals.*

☐ *Make at least one connection this week between what you've read in the Bible and what you've experienced in your daily life.*

☐ *Read an editorial in the newspaper and see if the writer's viewpoint expresses God's wisdom or the world's wisdom.*

Things to Remember

If any of you lack wisdom, you should pray to God, who will give it to you; because God gives generously and graciously to all.

JAMES 1:5 GNT

Happy is the person who finds wisdom, the one who gets understanding. Wisdom is worth more than silver; it brings more profit than gold. Wisdom is more precious than rubies; nothing you could want is equal to it.

PROVERBS 3:13–15 NCV

The words of good people are wise,
and they are always fair.
Psalm 37:30 GNT

Oh, the depth of the riches both of the wisdom and knowledge of God! How unsearchable are His judgments and unfathomable His ways!

ROMANS 11:33 NASB

The fear of the LORD is the beginning of wisdom,
and the knowledge of the Holy One is understanding.

PROVERBS 9:10 NKJV

Don't fool yourselves. Suppose some of you think you are wise by the standards of the world. Then you should become a "fool" so that you can become wise. The wisdom of this world is foolishness in God's eyes. It is written, "God catches wise people in their own tricks."

1 CORINTHIANS 3:18–19 NIrV

In the same way, wisdom is pleasing to you. If you find it, you have hope for the future, and your wishes will come true.

PROVERBS 24:14 NCV

The wisdom from above is first pure, then peaceable, gentle, reasonable, full of mercy and good fruits, unwavering, without hypocrisy.

JAMES 3:17 NASB

You desire truth in the inward parts, and in the hidden part You will make me to know wisdom.

PSALM 51:6 NKJV

The LORD gives wisdom; from his mouth come knowledge and understanding.

PROVERBS 2:6 NRSV

Some folks are wise and some otherwise.

JOSH BILLINGS

Wise men still seek Him today.

DAN BELL

Knowledge is proud that he has learned so much; wisdom is humble that he knows no more.

WILLIAM COWPER

Knowledge comes by taking things apart. But wisdom comes by putting things together.

JOHN A. MORRISON

Where Do I Go from Here?

I know that nothing is better for them than to rejoice, and to do good in their lives, and also that every man should eat and drink and enjoy the good of all his labor—it is the gift of God.

ECCLESIASTES 3:12–13 NKJV

Sheila always knew she wanted to be a doctor. She refined that goal a few times, finally settling on a career in obstetrics. Joel had planned to join the family business after he earned his MBA. Before entering graduate school, he had a change of heart and decided to pursue a career in the Air Force. Heather watched her two classmates over the years with a twinge of envy. She had lots of interests but no career goals—not when she graduated from high school, not even when she graduated from college with a degree in history.

Three graduates, three very different experiences. Whether you're certain what career you want to pursue or you've already changed your mind once or twice or you have no clear direction, as a graduate you are facing countless questions about your future. Some are practical: Do you have enough money (or will you make enough money) to live on? Some are urgent: Three companies have offered you a job; which one should you take? Some, however, are extremely important but often go unasked: Is this really what God wants for you? Is this your heart's desire, or are you just out to make a lot of money? Will your plans contribute to the good of society?

Make a list of all those practical, urgent, and extremely important concerns that you have. Turn each item into a question to ask God. Write down the answers that you believe He is giving you; take time and don't attempt to rush God. Over the coming days, weeks, and even months, be alert to anything that appears to lead in a certain direction. Pray about everything that seems to point toward a specific future for you.

The Bible assures you that confusion does not come from God (1 Corinthians 14:33). If you're feeling confused about your career choice, ask Him to give you clarity. It's not unusual for graduates to question the path they've chosen for their future. You can trust that as long as you are on right terms with God—that you want to do His will and are willing to obey Him—then He will open every door of opportunity for you. Those doors may lead you to the career you've been preparing for, or they may lead to an entirely different future. You can rest assured that whatever skills and knowledge you have acquired so far will be put to use regardless of the path you pursue.

I Will

Trust God with every aspect of my future. _____ yes   _____ no

Carefully consider the important questions that apply to my career choice. _____ yes   _____ no

Be confident that God will give me clarity about my future. _____ yes   _____ no

Be prepared for God to change my direction. _____ yes   _____ no

Recognize the value of all the skills and knowledge I have acquired so far. _____ yes   _____ no

Give my confusion to God. _____ yes   _____ no

Be willing to obey God, no matter where He leads me. _____ yes   _____ no

Things to Do

☐ *Make a list of all of the concerns you have about your future—practical, urgent, and extremely important.*

☐ *Pray over your list and write down the answers God gives you.*

☐ *Discuss your concerns with your parents and an instructor, counselor, mentor, or pastor.*

☐ *Decide that until God gives you clear direction, you will not dismiss any of your options, such as college, grad school, military, self-employment, traditional job, or the mission field.*

☐ *Thank God that you have options to choose from.*

☐ *Work at whatever God has placed before you now instead of idly waiting for the perfect opportunity to come your way.*

Things to Remember

Lord our God, may your blessings be with us. Give us success in all we do!

PSALM 90:17 GNT

A man can't do anything better than eat and drink and be satisfied with his work. I'm finally seeing that those things also come from the hand of God.

ECCLESIASTES 2:24 NIrV

If you used to rob, you must stop robbing and start working, in order to earn an honest living for yourself and to be able to help the poor.

EPHESIANS 4:28 GNT

Then He said to His disciples, "The harvest truly is plentiful, but the laborers are few. Therefore pray the Lord of the harvest to send out laborers into His harvest."

MATTHEW 9:37–38 NKJV

Now listen, you who say, "Today or tomorrow we will go to this or that city. We will spend a year there. We will buy and sell and make money." You don't even know what will happen tomorrow. What is your life? It is a mist that appears for a little while. Then it disappears.

JAMES 4:13–14 NIrV

Make yourself indispensable, and you will move up. Act as though you are indispensable, and you will move out.

JULES ORMONT

The driving force of a career must come from the individual. Remember: Jobs are owned by the company, you own your career!

EARL NIGHTINGALE

Choices

Never-Ending Options

Trust in the LORD with all your heart, and lean not on your own understanding. In all your ways acknowledge Him, and He shall direct your paths.

PROVERBS 3:5–6 NKJV

Of all the milestones in your life, graduation marks the time when you gain greater freedom to make your own decisions. That's not to say you didn't have to make a lot of decisions when you were in school, but now—well, life seems to consist of a never-ending stream of options. How can you expect to make all the right choices?

Accept the fact that you will make some wrong decisions. Then figure out how to reduce the number of bad choices you make, and the number of good decisions you make should outnumber the bad ones. Just as important, your wrong choices will be of the inconsequential variety, like buying a brand of toothpaste that fails to deliver that just-brushed tingle to your mouth.

How can you increase the chances that you'll make wise decisions? You can begin by taking advantage of every decision-making resource available, starting with the Word of God. Thinking of renting an apartment with someone you don't know that well? Read what the Bible says about things like relationships and trustworthiness. Can't decide which church to attend? Check out the book of Acts and the instructions given to churches in Paul's epistles to discover what kind of church life pleases God. Many Bibles include reference pages that can help you find relevant verses. In addition, there are loads of biblical resources in libraries and on the Internet, such as the Bible study tools on crosswalk.com, Biblegateway.com, and Gospelcom.net. Pray that God will give you discernment and that His Spirit will guide you toward the right decisions.

Consider all the other resources available to you: the counsel of friends and leaders; the advice of your parents; the wisdom of Christian writers whose books can help you see certain issues more clearly; and that one ever-reliable factor you might try to ignore—your gut feeling. You can probably remember a time when you went ahead and did something that turned out to be disastrous, even though you knew deep down in your gut—also known as your conscience—that it was the wrong thing to do. Don't let that happen again. Some call that gut feeling a "check in your spirit." It's a momentary hesitation that you need to pay attention to.

God has provided everything you need to make sound choices. As you mature He will add to the resources available to you—including the wisdom that He alone can give. Draw on that wisdom, and your options won't seem so daunting anymore.

I Will

Expect God to help me make the right decisions. _____ yes _____ no

Learn from the bad choices I make. _____ yes _____ no

Rely on the Word of God and His Spirit for guidance. _____ yes _____ no

Understand that the Bible has answers for the
everyday decisions I have to make. _____ yes _____ no

Respond to God's leading when I sense a "check" in
my spirit. _____ yes _____ no

Draw on the wisdom of God and the counsel of
godly people. _____ yes _____ no

Be thankful for the many sources of help that God
has placed my life. _____ yes _____ no

Things to Do

☐ Decide right now that your first course of action will always be to
consult with God.

☐ List the major decisions you need to make in the near future. Entrust
the list to God.

☐ Write down the names, phone numbers, and email addresses of
everyone who can help you make a wise decision. Keep the list in your
Bible—and use it.

☐ Using an online concordance, a reference work that lists every Bible
verse in which a specific word is found, find the verses that will help
you make the right choices.

☐ Think of the last time you made a bad decision and figure out what
that experience taught you.

Things to Remember

You, LORD, are all I have, and you give me all I need; my future is in your hands. How wonderful are your gifts to me; how good they are!

PSALM 16:5-6 GNT

In your heart you plan your life. But the LORD decides where your steps will take you.

PROVERBS 16:9 NIrV

[Moses said to the Israelites,] "I call heaven and earth as witnesses today against you, that I have set before you life and death, blessing and cursing; therefore choose life, that both you and your descendants may live."

DEUTERONOMY 30:19 NKJV

[Joshua said to the Israelites,] "But suppose you don't want to serve him. Then choose for yourselves right now whom you will serve. You can choose the gods your people served east of the Euphrates River. Or you can choose the gods the Amorites serve. After all, you are living in their land. But as for me and my family, we will serve the LORD."

JOSHUA 24:15 NIrV

Man's power of choice enables him to think like an angel or a devil, a king or a slave. Whatever he chooses, mind will create and manifest.

FREDERICK BAILES

Between two evils, choose neither; between two goods, choose both.

TRYON EDWARDS

Communication

Words to the Wise

The heart of this people has become dull, and with their ears they scarcely hear, and they have closed their eyes; lest they should see with their eyes, and hear with their ears, and understand with their heart and return, and I should heal them.

ACTS 28:27 NASB

Christmas break was finally here. The last few days had been little more than a blur as Dave crammed for finals and got together the stuff he would need for the next month at home. His parents had planned to pick him up, but a note on the college bulletin board from someone who lived in his hometown had caught his eye. For the cost of a tank of gas, Dave could ride home with a guy named Josh.

That seemed like a good idea. Dave called the number on the note and found that Josh lived across town. They decided to meet halfway, at the gas station off exit 12 on the bypass, so Dave asked a buddy to give him a ride to the station.

Arriving a half hour or so late, Dave didn't think that

52 Checklist for Life *for Graduates*

would be much of a problem. But Josh wasn't there. As he dug through his pockets for Josh's cell number, his own phone rang. "Where are you?" Josh demanded. "I need to get on the road *now*." "I'm at the gas station at exit 12, like you said," Dave replied. "No you're not. *I'm* at the station, and there's no one else here," an irritated Josh answered.

It turned out that Josh was waiting at the BP station on the north side of the bypass, while Dave and his buddy were at the Texaco on the south side. An overpass blocked each other's view. Eventually they got together, but the ride home was a tense one, with Josh pushing the speed limit all the way.

For a society that has so many means of communication at its disposal—landline and cell phones, email, pagers, fax machines, and mail services—communication still poses many problems. The problems are far more serious than Josh and Dave's mix-up.

Each person brings to even the most ordinary conversation a history in which words carry different meanings. For example, the problem with Josh and Dave stemmed not only from Josh's failure to be specific—"the gas station" turned out to be too general a description—but also from Josh's history. Coming from a small, one-gas-station town, Josh got so used to calling the BP station by its generic equivalent that it didn't occur to him that Dave would not have that same frame of reference.

In that situation everything got sorted out. Too often, misunderstandings don't clear up that easily, if at all. Learning to communicate effectively can help you avoid misunderstandings today and in the coming years, when you will be faced with postgraduation job interviews and on-the-job experiences like nothing you have ever known before. As with everything else in life, it's best to begin the learning process with God, whose words created an entire world.

Ask God to show you how you can become a better speaker—how you can convey your thoughts, feelings, and ideas to other people in a way that clearly communicates what you want them to know. Stop and think about what you're going to say before you open your mouth; make sure your words are unambiguous.

Pay close attention to the way good communicators speak and learn from their example. Pastors are generally good communicators, and yours may serve as a great example of the kind of skill it takes to clearly and accurately get ideas across to other people.

As you venture out into the world, you'll find that effective communication could prevent a host of problems. Let the Creator of all communication be the Lord of your conversations. You can trust the One who invented language to help you use it in a clear and edifying way.

I Will

	yes	no
Ask God to guard my speech.		
Learn how to become a better communicator.		
Eliminate habits, like interrupting, that are discourteous.		
Take care never to say hurtful things to others.		
Avoid preparing a response until I've give thoughtful attention to the words of others.		
Make sure the conversations I have with others are pleasing to God.		

Things to Do

☐ *Think of a recent misunderstanding you had with a friend or parent, and see how better communication on your part could have prevented the problem.*

☐ *Over the next week, make a note of how many times you interrupt other people. Resolve to interrupt less frequently.*

☐ *Write down clear and specific directions to your house, dorm, or apartment from several major highways or well-known landmarks, for the benefit of others.*

☐ *Watch several TV sitcoms, noting how often poor communication on the part of the speaker figures into the plotlines.*

☐ *Ask God to help you learn to express your thoughts more clearly.*

Things to Remember

It is the same with you. Unless you speak clearly with your tongue, no one can understand what you are saying. You will be talking into the air!

1 CORINTHIANS 14:9 NCV

Put away perversity from your mouth; keep corrupt talk far from your lips.

PROVERBS 4:24 NIV

Don't waste your breath on fools, for they will despise the wisest advice.
Proverbs 23:9 NLT

And pleasant speech increases persuasiveness.

PROVERBS 16:21 NRSV

Speak and act as those who are going to be judged by the law that gives freedom.

JAMES 2:12 NIV

Let the words of my mouth and the meditation of my heart be acceptable in Your sight, O LORD, my rock and my Redeemer.

PSALM 19:14 NASB

[Jesus told His disciples,] "When they bring you before the synagogues and the rulers and the authorities, do not become anxious about how or what you should speak in your defense, or what you are to say; for the Holy Spirit will teach you in that very hour what you ought to say."

LUKE 12:11–12 NASB

Sin is unavoidable when there is much talk, but whoever seals his lips is wise.

PROVERBS 10:19 GOD'S WORD

Those who are sure of themselves do not talk all the time. People who stay calm have real insight.

PROVERBS 17:27 GNT

Let your speech always be with grace, seasoned with salt, that you may know how you ought to answer each one.

COLOSSIANS 4:6 NKJV

Two monologues do not make a dialogue.
JEFF DALY

There cannot be greater rudeness than to interrupt another in the current of his discourse.
JOHN LOCKE

Competition

Ungodly Games

Everyone who competes for the prize is temperate in all things. Now they do it to obtain a perishable crown, but we for an imperishable crown.

1 CORINTHIANS 9:25 NKJV

As an all-star linebacker on his high school football team, Jerome faced some exceedingly tough competition—guys who were bigger and meaner and even tougher than he was. Like lots of athletes, Jerome carried the spirit of competition that he had honed on the playing field over to his academic and personal life as well. He was doing all right for himself, getting ahead both on and off the field. After he graduated, he discovered that he was facing the toughest competition of his life—the rough play sometimes found in the world of corporate business.

Like Jerome, you may be thrown off guard when you come up against some of the fiercest competitors you can possibly imagine. While most of your coworkers, colleagues, or fellow college students will generally be decent people, you should prepare yourself to handle the machinations of those few whose driving ambition results in a complete disregard for the damage it inflicts on others. You need to be on the lookout for their tactics, both obvious and subtle, but most of all you need to guard against the temptation to participate in their competitive games.

Ask God to keep your motives pure and your eyes on the ultimate goal, an imperishable crown. Pray for Him to give you His love for the fierce competitors in your life, those who right now can see only material gain. Then turn your prayerful attention toward them; pray that their hearts will be turned toward Him and that He will give them wisdom for today and a glimpse of the possibility of an eternal future in the presence of God Himself.

What can you do in addition to praying for your coworkers? You can look for God-given opportunities to carefully show them, by your example, that there's a better way to live and work. You may not be ready to become close friends with those who seem to work against you. Cutthroat people are often understandably friendless and lonely, and you should always maintain a friendly attitude toward them. Your smile may be the only genuine one they see all day.

Above all, keep that eternal goal line ever before you. Make sure you are always playing on the right field, the one God wants you to be on, and make sure you play fair. When you cross that goal line into eternity, there will be a victor's crown awaiting you.

I Will

Compete for the prize of an imperishable crown.

yes _____ _no_ _____

Ask God to help me keep my motives pure.

yes _____ _no_ _____

Provide an example of godly work habits to others.

yes _____ _no_ _____

Maintain a friendly attitude toward my competitors.

yes _____ _no_ _____

Rely on God to protect me from those who may be out to hurt me.

yes _____ _no_ _____

Refuse to be drawn into ungodly competitive games.

yes _____ _no_ _____

Things to Do

☐ _Ask God to keep you from developing an ungodly spirit of competition._

☐ _Make a list of the ways that you can model godly competition for others._

☐ _Recall an example of appropriate competition that you've witnessed or experienced, and determine what you can learn from it._

☐ _Pray that God will steady your focus on the eternal goal line._

☐ _Memorize 1 Corinthians 9:25, focusing on the imperishable crown that awaits you._

☐ _List ways you can achieve your goals without resorting to unfair competition, such as striving for excellence and competing only against yourself._

Things to Remember

Be kindly affectionate to one another with brotherly love, in honor giving preference to one another.

ROMANS 12:10 NKJV

You will understand what is right and just and fair—every good path.

PROVERBS 2:9 NIV

In the same way, anyone who takes part in a sport doesn't receive the winner's crown unless he plays by the rules.

2 TIMOTHY 2:5 NIrV

[Jesus said,] "I do not pray for these alone, but also for those who will believe in Me through their word; that they all may be one, as You, Father, are in Me, and I in You; that they also may be one in Us, that the world may believe that You sent Me."

JOHN 17:20–21 NKJV

He is the Rock. His work is perfect. Everything he does is just and fair. He is faithful, without sin.

DEUTERONOMY 32:4 TLB

The Law of Win/Win says, "Let's not do it your way or my way; let's do it the best way."

GREG ANDERSON

Focus on competition has always been a formula for mediocrity.

DANIEL BURRUS

Constructive Criticism

Compassionate Response

If you listen to constructive criticism, you will be at home among the wise.

PROVERBS 15:31 NLT

Jenna had a problem, and to her, it was a big one. She had graduated at the end of May, and, having decided to continue her education, she had more than three full months between then and Labor Day to earn a good portion of the money she would need throughout the upcoming academic year. She landed a terrific temporary job, but a week into it she could hardly stand the thought of working there all summer. She had nothing but complaints about her "incompetent" boss—his gruff manner, the little training he gave her, the way he favored the permanent employees. Most of these complaints she voiced to her good friend Tara.

"You know, Jenna, I've always thought of you as a prayer warrior. You're so fortunate that you have such a strong prayer life," Tara said during yet another phone call filled with complaints about Jenna's job. "You could sure take advantage of that right now."

Tara's response is a great example of an honest but

kind and subtle form of constructive criticism. Had her response been expressed negatively ("You really ought to quit complaining and start praying, like you're always telling other people to do"), she would have lost a valuable opportunity to build up Jenna's faith and help her turn the situation around.

Kindness is perhaps the key element that separates constructive criticism from negative criticism. When your comments flow from a heart filled with compassion, your words become attractive to others. Imagine how Jenna felt after that phone conversation. Instead of feeling belittled or berated, she probably felt strengthened and encouraged to do what she knew she should do all along: Stop complaining about her boss and lay the situation out before the Lord in prayer.

Learning to handle a situation the way Tara did requires a healthy reliance on God for both wisdom and the discipline to avoid a destructively critical attitude. As a believer you have access to God's Spirit, and you can rely on Him to give you a right attitude. However, it is important to remember that not everyone you meet in life will be as gracious and tactful as you have learned to be. Learn to accept the good with the bad: the constructive criticism that is based on kindness and compassion and good intentions, and the ineptly delivered or mean-spirited negative criticism. Just make sure that you deliver only one type, the kind that flows from a heart filled with compassion.

I Will

Encourage others to exercise their areas of spiritual strength, such as Jenna's prayer life.

yes ___ no ___

Remember that kindness is the hallmark of constructive criticism.

yes ___ no ___

Maintain a heart that is filled with compassion for others.

yes ___ no ___

Accept the criticism of others with grace.

yes ___ no ___

Keep my critical attitude in check.

yes ___ no ___

Depend on God to teach me how to be tactful.

yes ___ no ___

Focus on building other people up instead of tearing them down.

yes ___ no ___

Things to Do

☐ *Recall a recent situation in which you criticized someone and determine how you could have handled it better.*

☐ *Ask God to teach you tactfulness.*

☐ *Examine your life in terms of the compassion you've exhibited lately.*

☐ *Memorize at least two of the accompanying scriptures about criticism.*

☐ *Choose someone you've been particularly critical of to place at the top of your prayer list.*

☐ *Pray for an extra measure of kindness in your words and your actions.*

Things to Remember

[Jesus said,] "Judge not, and you shall not be judged. Condemn not, and you shall not be condemned. Forgive, and you will be forgiven."

LUKE 6:37 NKJV

You can offer no excuse, O man, whoever indulges in judging; for by passing judgment on another you condemn yourself, since you, who are passing judgment practice the same things.

ROMANS 2:1 MLB

Tell them not to speak evil of anyone, but to be peaceful and friendly, and always to show a gentle attitude toward everyone.

TITUS 3:2 GNT

[Jesus said,] "Blessed are you when men hate you, and when they exclude you, and revile you, and cast out your name as evil, for the Son of Man's sake."

LUKE 6:22 NKJV

My brothers and sisters, don't speak against one another. Anyone who speaks against another believer speaks against the law. And anyone who judges another believer judges the law. When you judge the law, you are not keeping it.

JAMES 4:11 NIrV

If what they are saying about you is true, mend your ways. If it isn't true, forget it, and go on and serve the Lord.

H. A. IRONSIDE

Honest criticism is hard to take, especially from a relative, a friend, an acquaintance, or a stranger.

FRANKLIN P. JONES

Grace

Freely Given

By grace you have been saved through faith, and that not of
yourselves; it is the gift of God, not of works, lest anyone
should boast.

EPHESIANS 2:8–9 NKJV

It started out like most practical jokes—a prank
cooked up in a dormitory suite when the late-spring
weather has been cold and rainy for a week. Five students,
under the influence of sleep deprivation and boredom-
induced cabin fever, thought it would be loads of fun to
rig up a contraption that would dump a bucketful of ice
water on the first person who left the suite next door in
the morning.

They could not have known that Cindi, who was
afflicted with a degenerative nerve disorder, had spent the
night next door cramming for pre-graduation finals with
her friend Glenna. They could not have known that she
would leave just after dawn, when she felt it would be safe
to return to her own dorm building—or that she would
slip and fall, breaking several bones in her already
disabled body. A prank that would have shocked and
bruised an able-bodied person resulted in serious injury to
Cindi.

The culprits were devastated. They all knew and liked Cindi, and had helped her at times when she needed to do things her body would not allow her to do. When Cindi was able to receive visitors at the hospital, the five students were the first ones there—that is, right after Cindi's parents, who had seen their daughter struggle for years, trying with great difficulty to do things that other people take for granted. As they sat with Cindi, stroking her hair and holding her hands, they looked up to see the very people who hurt their daughter walk in the room.

At the sight of Cindi's parents, one of the students stammered out an apology and fled the room with the other four, who were too stunned to speak. "Wait!" they heard a man say, and turned to find Cindi's father coming after them. Shamed, frightened, and close to tears, the students were unprepared for what he said next. "Look, this has been hard for Cindi's mother and me, but it's been hard for you too. After Glenna explained what happened and how you were taking this, we called the college and asked them not to put you on probation. We know that you realize what you did was wrong, and we think you've suffered enough punishment. We'll get Cindi through this. Right now, I think she'd like to see you and tell you herself that it's all going to be OK."

That is grace in action, a real-life example of what it's like to have God grant mercy to you when you've blown it. You deserve punishment; He gives you grace by showering His favor on you when you least expect it. The cross of Christ, of course, is the ultimate example of grace; through the cross God gave you the gift of eternal life at the price of His Son's life. Jesus took the punishment that you—and everyone else—deserved.

Over the course of two millennia, God has extended His offer of the free gift of grace not only to people whose hearts may have already been inclined toward Him but also to those people who rejected Him and rebelled against Him and treated Him with the utmost contempt. There wasn't a single thing they could do to earn His favor.

You can't earn His favor, either, but there is a lot you can do to show Him how much you appreciate His overwhelmingly kind gift. First and foremost, accept it. Then thank Him and show your gratitude by being obedient to Him and His word. Spend time with Him daily, getting to know Him and allowing Him to continue to minister to you. Find ways to serve Him. Find ways to serve others and tell them about this awesome gift God has given you and has made available to them as well.

Is all that necessary? No, but it's the appropriate response of a genuinely grateful person toward the One who could have unleashed His wrath but released His kindness instead.

Accept God's generous offer with humility. Never take it for granted. Never think there's anything you have to do to earn it.

God grants grace freely, and He wants you to enjoy it just as freely. Show your enjoyment by striving to please Him in all you say and do. When you think about it, that's a pretty good deal.

I Will

Thank God for His incredible gift of grace.   _yes_   _no_

Show my gratitude for the favor He has shown me.   _yes_   _no_

Strive to please God in all that I say and do.   _yes_   _no_

Understand that I cannot earn God's grace.   _yes_   _no_

Share the good news of God's grace with others.   _yes_   _no_

Accept God's offer of grace with humility.   _yes_   _no_

Be careful not to take His grace for granted.   _yes_   _no_

Things to Do

☐ _Choose three verses about grace listed on these pages and memorize them._

☐ _Write out an explanation of grace that a child would understand._

☐ _Find a news story about a judge's decision that illustrates the concept of grace._

☐ _Read the parable of the Prodigal Son (Luke 15:11–32) to see how the father applied the concept of grace._

☐ _Think of a time when your parents or someone else extended grace to you and thank them for it._

☐ _Write a letter to God, thanking Him for His grace and telling Him what it has meant in your life._

Things to Remember

If he chose them by grace, it is not for the things they have done. If they could be made God's people by what they did, God's gift of grace would not really be a gift.

ROMANS 11:6 NCV

We believe that through the grace of the Lord Jesus Christ we shall be saved in the same manner as they.

ACTS 15:11 NKJV

He gives us more grace. That is why Scripture says: "God opposes the proud but gives grace to the humble."
James 4:6 NIV

When they had performed everything according to the Law of the Lord, they returned to Galilee, to their own city of Nazareth. And the Child continued to grow and become strong, increasing in wisdom; and the grace of God was upon Him.

LUKE 2:39–40 NASB

God's saving grace has appeared to all people. It teaches us to say no to godless ways and sinful longings. We must control ourselves. We must do what is right. We must lead godly lives in today's world.

TITUS 2:11–12 NIrV

From the fullness of his grace we have all received one blessing after another. For the law was given through Moses; grace and truth came through Jesus Christ.

JOHN 1:16–17 NIV

In Christ we are set free by the blood of his death, and so we have forgiveness of sins. How rich is God's grace, which he has given to us so fully and freely. God, with full wisdom and understanding, let us know his secret purpose. This was what God wanted, and he planned to do it through Christ.

EPHESIANS 1:7–9 NCV

Since we have been justified through faith, we have peace with God through our Lord Jesus Christ, through whom we have gained access by faith into this grace in which we now stand. And we rejoice in the hope of the glory of God.

ROMANS 5:1–2 NIV

God is able to make all grace abound toward you, that you, always having all sufficiency in all things, may have an abundance for every good work.

2 CORINTHIANS 9:8 NKJV

Grace means the free, unmerited, unexpected love of God, and all the benefits, delights, and comforts which flow from it. It means that while we were sinners and enemies we have been treated as sons and heirs.

R. P. C. HANSON

Grace is free sovereign favor to the ill-deserving.

BENJAMIN B. WARFIELD

Corruption

Downward Spiral

Do not be deceived: "Evil company corrupts good habits."

1 CORINTHIANS 15:33 NKJV

Imagine finding yourself imprisoned for a crime you didn't commit. Your only hope of getting out is a widely used action—bribing a highly placed official. What would you do? Hand over the money or languish in jail for years? That's the dilemma the apostle Paul faced when a corrupt Roman official named Felix had him imprisoned—even though Felix was convinced of Paul's innocence (see Acts 24). Over the next two years, Paul had many opportunities to bribe Felix to release him, but he chose to remain in prison rather than contribute to corruption.

Some might consider Paul's decision to be foolish. Why not think of the bribe as bail? Couldn't he have done more good as a free man than as an inmate? What's the big deal, anyway? The big deal—one that Paul understood well—is the nature of corruption. Corruption is sin, of course, but not all sin is corruption. Accepting an illegal bribe is sin; becoming so accustomed to accepting bribes that you no longer care whether it is sin is corruption. It's a degenerative process, a downward spiral of deliberate, sinful activity, and it's nearly always rooted in greed.

What does this have to do with you? On campus a student who can tap into a "secure" area of the college's Web site offers to show you how to do it—for a price. On the job a coworker responsible for confidential data says you can take a peek at it in exchange for the private phone numbers in your files. On a military base someone boasts that he can help you circumvent the rules by greasing the palms of a certain officer. If you were to participate in any of those transactions, you would be contributing to corruption even if you were not the instigator.

Corruption is insidious because it can become so easy to rationalize. In Paul's situation the Roman Empire had become so corrupt that bribery was simply another method of doing business. Paul refused to buy into it. He knew that a seemingly isolated act of corruption can turn into a sinful habit, with severe consequences.

You need to deal with sin immediately, before it threatens to corrupt you. Listen to that still small voice, the one that reminds you to confess your sin and accept God's forgiveness (1 John 1:9). As you walk in the forgiveness of God, you can do so knowing that by acknowledging and turning from sin, you have avoided the downward spiral that results in corruption.

I Will

Remember that rationalized sin is still sin. _yes_ _no_

Confess my sin immediately before it has a chance to grow. _yes_ _no_

Trust God to be with me when I take a stand against corruption. _yes_ _no_

Believe that God is faithful and just to forgive my sins. _yes_ _no_

Determine to turn away from anything that tempts me to do wrong. _yes_ _no_

Be sensitive to the still small voice inside of me. _yes_ _no_

Things to Do

☐ *Read the account of Felix and Paul's encounter in Acts 24.*

☐ *Examine your heart for any unconfessed sin in your life right now and confess it to God.*

☐ *Thank God that He has provided a way for you to deal with specific sins before they become a degenerative habit.*

☐ *Find a newspaper or online news story about a recent corruption case, noting the sin involved.*

☐ *Read the Thoreau quotation and resolve to never have your goodness tainted by corruption.*

☐ *Watch the classic 1966 film* A Man for All Seasons, *which depicts Sir Thomas More's stand against the corrupt Henry VIII.*

Things to Remember

Through [his glory and goodness] he gave us the very great and precious promises. With these gifts you can share in being like God, and the world will not ruin you with its evil desires.

2 PETER 1:4 NCV

The fool has said in his heart, "There is no God." They are corrupt, they have committed abominable deeds; there is no one who does good.

PSALM 14:1 NASB

You were told that your foolish desires will destroy you and that you must give up your old way of life with all its bad habits. Let the Spirit change your way of thinking.

EPHESIANS 4:22–23 CEV

If we confess our sins, He is faithful and just to forgive us our sins and to cleanse us from all unrighteousness.

1 JOHN 1:9 NKJV

While [the ungodly] promise [those who have escaped from sin] liberty, they themselves are slaves of corruption; for by whom a person is overcome, by him also he is brought into bondage.

2 PETER 2:19 NKJV

There is no odor so bad as that which arises from goodness tainted.

HENRY DAVID THOREAU

Corruption is like a ball of snow; once it's set a-rolling it must increase.

CHARLES CALEB COLTON

Courage

Moral Valor

In all these things we overwhelmingly conquer through Him who loved us.

ROMANS 8:37 NASB

A freshman at a major university, Sarina seemed to be well-liked. Her suite mates in the dorm realized she wasn't interested in partying with them, but they shrugged it off and pegged her as the bookish type. That wasn't entirely true, but no one had questioned her further, and she had not volunteered to share her faith with them.

Everything changed one day during a discussion in class about the sexual tension in a nineteenth-century novel when Sarina's classmates seemed at a loss to understand why *this* character didn't just go to bed with *that* character and get it over with. Sarina pointed out that the characters were devout in their faith and wanted to please God by resisting temptation. A spirited argument ensued; one student denounced the novel as irrelevant due to its antiquated moral message. "Anyway, no one really believes the Bible anymore," he added. "I do," Sarina quietly said, after several students turned to see how she would respond. Suddenly, the students' attention was no longer on the novel but on Sarina. When they challenged her further, she said she believed biblical morality to be timeless rather than old-fashioned.

When you think of courage, the first thing that comes to your mind is probably not a young woman in a college classroom. You might think of a character in an action-packed movie or the passengers who lost their lives diverting a hijacked plane away from the nation's capital. Sarina's actions in class that day were no less courageous. Hers was the lone dissenting voice in a classroom of skeptical and mocking peers. Taking an unpopular stand, one that you know will result in ridicule and stereotyping, requires a considerable measure of courage. Sarina's dependence on the Holy Spirit enabled her to confidently express her beliefs with grace.

Challenges to your beliefs are inevitable. How will you handle them when you are surrounded by unfamiliar faces in a college classroom, military barracks, or employee lunchroom? Never, ever enter those areas—or any other— without the Holy Spirit. You may be walking right into a spiritual trap designed to immobilize you in your attempts to express your beliefs. When you walk in the power of the Spirit of God, you can rely on the Spirit of God to give you the words, the confidence, and the courage you need to defend your convictions in the face of spiritual opposition.

I Will

Maintain my biblical convictions in the face of opposition.

yes _no_

Rely on the Holy Spirit to embolden me when my beliefs are challenged.

yes _no_

Have the courage to resist intense peer pressure.

yes _no_

Realize that ridicule and mockery may result when I take a courageous stand.

yes _no_

Learn to see myself as an overwhelming conqueror.

yes _no_

Support my friends when their faith is challenged.

yes _no_

Realize that I can have confidence in the timeless truth of Scripture.

yes _no_

Things to Do

☐ _Ask God's Spirit to begin preparing you now for the next challenge to your faith._

☐ _Read the story of Shadrach, Meshach, and Abednego in Daniel 3, paying particular attention to verses 17–18._

☐ _Thank God for His promise to make you as bold as a lion (Proverbs 28:1)._

☐ _Think of the last time your courage was tested and analyze how you handled the situation in light of biblical truth._

☐ _Pray Psalm 138 back to God._

☐ _Read Jesus Freaks by dc Talk or another good book about Christians who took courageous stands for their faith._

Things to Remember

We can go to God with bold confidence through faith in Christ.

EPHESIANS 3:12 GOD'S WORD

But you, mortal man, must not be afraid of them or of anything they say. They will defy and despise you; it will be like living among scorpions. Still, don't be afraid of those rebels or of anything they say.

EZEKIEL 2:6 GNT

The LORD will be your confidence, and will keep your foot from being caught.

PROVERBS 3:26 NASB

The wicked run away when no one is chasing them, but the godly are as bold as lions.

PROVERBS 28:1 NLT

Be of good courage, and He shall strengthen your heart, all you who hope in the LORD.

PSALM 31:24 NKJV

Courage is fear that has said its prayers.

DOROTHY BERNARD

Facing it, always facing it, that's the way to get through. Face it.

JOSEPH CONRAD

Leaving Home

On Your Own

The LORD shall preserve you from all evil; He shall preserve your soul. The Lord shall preserve your going out and your coming in from this time forth, and even forevermore.

PSALM 121:7–8 NKJV

As the day neared when Melissa would be starting a new life in a new city, things at home started to get tense. Her parents, who had always trusted her, were suddenly questioning her about everything—where she went, what she did, who she was with. Why did she have to go out so much, anyway?

Meanwhile, her sister began tailing her the way she had when they were much younger. That used to annoy Melissa, but in recent years, she and Ashley—who was only a year younger—had become as much friends as they were sisters. Now, Ashley was like her shadow, except that she talked pretty much all the time, peppering Melissa with questions about things like what stuff she was taking with her and what she was leaving behind.

This was starting to get on Melissa's nerves. With a

million things of her own to think about, she didn't need this grand inquisition. At the start of the summer two months earlier her family had seemed so normal. Now they were acting really weird, by Melissa's standards. Sure, she knew they weren't looking forward to her departure; she was moving halfway across the country, and she probably wouldn't be able to get home until Thanksgiving, if then. Really, couldn't they understand how excited she was about her plans? Couldn't they show some enthusiastic support for her?

What was happening in Melissa's family was far from "weird," and deep down, Melissa knew that. She knew that everyone—herself included—was having a hard time adjusting to the idea of her leaving home. It was much easier for Melissa to focus on the excitement she felt and the details she needed to handle than to think about her own uneasiness at going off on her own.

As you face this major change in your life, your family may behave much like Melissa's. If your parents become more inquisitive about how you are spending your last few weeks at home, it may be because they are making one last attempt at reminding you of the Christian values they want you to take with you. They understandably want to spend more time with you as well, knowing how long it will be until they see you again.

If you have younger siblings, they are also trying to adjust to the idea that big brother or big sister will no longer be there. On the surface Ashley's questions may appear to be selfishly motivated *(If Melissa isn't taking her television, then I can have it)*, but that may not be the case at all. The more Melissa leaves behind, the more likely it is that she will return some day.

That's an assurance Ashley—and possibly your own brother or sister—needs.

All this tension at home, coupled with your own inner turmoil about the changes you are facing, is keeping you from enjoying the time you have left at home. Sit down with each member of your family individually and talk about what's going on—but before you do, you need to spend time in prayer, asking God to prepare their hearts, to give you wisdom about what you are going to say, and to make sure you say it all in the right spirit. Ask Him to help you see your departure from everyone else's perspective.

Assure your parents that you love them, that you will miss them, and that you have every intention of adhering to the standards they have instilled in you since birth. Remind them that you need some space—that this move is difficult for you as well, that you have many things on your mind, and the tension at home is getting to you. Then talk to your siblings. Express your love, remind them that you can keep in touch by e-mail, and tell them you will come home as soon as you can.

Remain sensitive to your family's feelings. Rely on God to help you find a balance between the time you spend with your family, your friends, and yourself. You can count on Him to be with you throughout this time of transition. You can have the confidence of knowing that you can add His presence to all those other things you'll be taking with you when you leave home.

I Will

Understand that my family is trying to adjust to
my departure.

yes _____ *no* _____

Depend on God to see us all through this time
of transition.

yes _____ *no* _____

Try to see this situation from everyone else's
perspective.

yes _____ *no* _____

Trust God to give me wisdom in dealing with my
family's emotions.

yes _____ *no* _____

Keep the lines of communication open with
my family.

yes _____ *no* _____

Things to Do

☐ *Make a point of giving something of yours to each of your siblings
before you leave.*

☐ *Ask God to release each person from the tension he or she is experiencing.*

☐ *Write a reassuring letter to your parents. Give it to them when you
leave.*

☐ *Keep a running list of things to do before you leave so your mind will
be free to deal with more important issues.*

☐ *Schedule a time to have a private talk with each member of your
family.*

☐ *Come up with two or three ideas for fun activities you can do with your
family before you move away.*

Things to Remember

Another said, "I'll follow you, sir, but first let me tell my family goodbye." Jesus said to him, "Whoever starts to plow and looks back is not fit for the kingdom of God."

LUKE 9:61–62 GOD'S WORD

Who among you fears the LORD and obeys his servant? If you are walking in darkness, without a ray of light, trust in the LORD and rely on your God.

ISAIAH 50:10 NLT

It is God who arms me with strength, and makes my way perfect.
Psalm 18:32 NKJV

Be to me a rock of habitation to which I may continually come; You have given commandment to save me, for You are my rock and my fortress.

PSALM 71:3 NASB

[The psalmist wrote,] You have made the LORD, my refuge, even the Most High, your dwelling place.

PSALM 91:9 NASB

Then he said to them all, "If any want to become my followers, let them deny themselves and take up their cross daily and follow me."

LUKE 9:23 NRSV

You will show me the path of life; in Your presence is fullness of joy; at Your right hand are pleasures forevermore.

PSALM 16:11 NKJV

God's way is perfect! The promise of the LORD has proven to be true. He is a shield to all those who take refuge in him.

PSALM 18:30 GOD'S WORD

It is good for me to draw near to God; I have put my trust in the LORD God, that I may declare all Your works.

PSALM 73:28 NKJV

How precious your faithful love is! Important and ordinary people alike find safety in the shadow of your wings.

PSALM 36:7 NIrV

Your word is a lamp to my feet and a light for my path.

PSALM 119:105 NIV

Home is the place where we are treated the best, but grumble the most.

ANONYMOUS

We carry our homes within us which enables us to fly.

JOHN CAGEX

Inventiveness

Created to Be Creative

[Paul said to the Athenians:] "In Him we live and move and have our being, as also some of your own poets have said, 'For we are also His offspring.'"

ACTS 17:28 NKJV

You have the potential to be creative, because God, the Creator of all, is the one who made you. He repeatedly assures you throughout the Bible that all He is and all He has is at your disposable. That includes creativity, the ability to express yourself in an original and imaginative way. Accessing that ability, though, is your responsibility.

One of the best things you can do to unearth the creative skills you already have is to make sure you understand how broad the range of creativity can be. If to you a creative person is an artist, and you can't draw very well, you might consider yourself to be creativity-challenged. If you've ever come up with a funny song to entertain the children you baby-sit, that's creativity at work. You may just have a hard time seeing it that way.

One of the good things about creativity is that you can

do a lot to enhance it. Be on the lookout for fresh and inventive ideas; build on the skills you already have by using your imagination and seeking out new sources of inspiration. Best of all, try something new and completely different. If you're a writer, take up pottery; if you're a watercolor artist, try black-and-white photography; if you're a Web site designer, take a drawing class. If you can't see any area in your life in which you consider yourself to be creative, read Psalm 139, which says you were "fearfully and wonderfully made" (verse 14) and "skillfully wrought in the lowest parts of the earth" (verse 15, both NKJV). Meditate on the creativity that went in to forming you, and believe that the Creator imparted something of His own creative ability to you. Then find an outlet for your hidden creativity.

Paul's first letter to the Corinthians says that if you are a genuine follower of Jesus, then you have the mind of Christ (1 Corinthians 2:16). His is the greatest creative mind that ever was. He wants you to draw on the depth of His creativity to inspire the people whose lives you touch to reach beyond their everyday existence and recognize the hand of God, the Creator. He is the driving creative force behind all that is and all that ever will be, and He wants you to be an instrument of that force on earth.

I Will

See myself as a creative person. _yes_ _no_

Recognize that all creativity comes from God. _yes_ _no_

Understand what creativity is. _yes_ _no_

Believe that I have the mind of Christ. _yes_ _no_

Strive to inspire others through the creativity God has given me. _yes_ _no_

Keep my mind and spirit fresh by trying new things. _yes_ _no_

Be grateful for the measure of creativity God has given me. _yes_ _no_

Things to Do

☐ *Visit an art gallery or folk art museum; slow down and see the creativity at work in the pieces on display.*

☐ *Pray Psalm 139 back to God.*

☐ *Take a class, borrow a book, or download instructions for a project in a creative field that's new to you.*

☐ *Watch a creative person at work, such as a woodworker, quilter, painter, or potter, and notice the care they take in their work.*

☐ *Ask God to show you how you can be an instrument of His creative force on earth.*

☐ *Do one thing to improve the creative skills you already have.*

Things to Remember

"For who has known the mind of the Lord so as to instruct him?" But we have the mind of Christ.

1 CORINTHIANS 2:16 NRSV

Christ is the one through whom God created everything in heaven and earth. He made the things we can see and the things we can't see—kings, kingdoms, rulers, and authorities. Everything has been created through him and for him.

COLOSSIANS 1:16 NLT

My heart overflows with a good theme; I address my verses to the King; my tongue is the pen of a ready writer.

PSALM 45:1 NASB

My God put the idea into my head that I should gather the nobles, leaders, and people so that they could check their genealogy. I found the book with the genealogy of those who came back the first time. I found the following written in it.

NEHEMIAH 7:5 GOD'S WORD

Brothers and sisters, think about the things that are good and worthy of praise. Think about the things that are true and honorable and right and pure and beautiful and respected.

PHILIPPIANS 4:8 NCV

A hunch is creativity trying to tell you something.

FRANK CAPRA

The essential part of creativity is not being afraid to fail.

EDWIN H. LAND

Dreams

Hidden in Your Heart

I will pour out My Spirit on all flesh; your sons and your daughters shall prophesy, your old men shall dream dreams, your young men shall see visions.

JOEL 2:28 NKJV

Have you ever dreamed a really big dream— something so big that only God could make it come to pass? If not, this is a great time to start. Graduation marks your transition toward a future of unlimited opportunities—especially as you place those opportunities in the hands of your eternal Father. He wants you to trust Him to do great things through you that will bring glory and honor to His name.

Try looking at your tangible, down-to-earth plans in light of the things you tend to dream about. Maybe your primary interest has been drama, but your mind keeps wandering back to the Guatemalan children you met on a short-term mission trip. Is God leading you into mission work instead? Maybe, but maybe not. You might be the person God wants to use to create a groundbreaking type of evangelistic outreach through dramatic performances.

Or maybe you're a computer nerd but you want to make a difference in the world. You may not be able to see any way that your plans to become a Web site designer can possibly change even a small corner of the world, but if that's a dream God has placed within your heart, you can be assured He will bring it to pass.

Dreams fire your imagination. They allow you to rise above the daily bombardment of noise and words and images and enable you to catch a glimpse of the endless possibilities for your future. Dreams are what thinking outside the box is all about. They encourage you to do the unexpected, unconventional thing. Bathe them with prayer; ask God to show you why you dream about the things you do. Ask God to help you refine your dreams, and above all, ask Him to reveal to you any dream you have that is not from Him. He can see what's hidden in your heart; He knows the dreams you dream, and He will gladly destroy any that are ungodly. Don't expect Him to fulfill your dream if what you want is to be idolized by millions of people.

The Bible says that if you delight in the Lord, He will give you the desires—the dreams—of your heart. If you truly delight in the Lord, your dreams will be pleasing to Him. Go ahead—dream big dreams. Expect to do great things for God and for others. Don't limit yourself to what you see right now. Give your expectations to God—and just watch Him transform them into a reality beyond your wildest dreams.

I Will

Allow God to bring glory and honor to His name by
doing great things through me.

yes _____ *no* _____

Believe that God can make my productive dreams
come true.

yes _____ *no* _____

Learn to dream big dreams.

yes _____ *no* _____

Stop dreaming about those things that are clearly
not from God.

yes _____ *no* _____

Bathe my hopes and aspirations in prayer.

yes _____ *no* _____

Delight in the Lord.

yes _____ *no* _____

Help my friends discover how God can help them
achieve their dreams.

yes _____ *no* _____

Things to Do

☐ *Make a list of the dreams for your life that you believe God has given
you. Pray about each item.*

☐ *Brainstorm with a friend about how each of you can combine your
dreams with your plans.*

☐ *Take one step—however small—toward making your dream come true.*

☐ *Ask the Holy Spirit to reveal to you any dreams that are not of God.*

☐ *Look at Goethe's quotation and dream about how you—yes, you—can
move the hearts of men and women.*

☐ *Thank God for allowing you to catch a glimpse of the endless
possibilities He has placed in your life.*

Things to Remember

The fears of the wicked will all come true; so will the hopes of the godly.

PROVERBS 10:24 NLT

Delight yourself also in the LORD, and He shall give you the desires of your heart.

PSALM 37:4 NKJV

I will give you a new heart and put a new spirit in you; I will remove from you your heart of stone and give you a heart of flesh.

EZEKIEL 36:26 NIV

The word of God is living and powerful, and sharper than any two-edged sword, piercing even to the division of soul and spirit, and of joints and marrow, and is a discerner of the thoughts and intents of the heart.

HEBREWS 4:12 NKJV

He said, "Listen to my words: 'When a prophet of the LORD is among you, I reveal myself to him in visions, I speak to him in dreams.'"

NUMBERS 12:6 NIV

We all have dreams. But in order to make dreams come into reality, it takes an awful lot of determination, dedication, self-discipline, and effort.

JESSE OWENS

Dream no small dreams for they have no power to move the hearts of men.

JOHANN WOLFGANG VON GOETHE

Family

Respectful but Independent

"Honor your father and mother"—which is the first commandment with a promise—"that it may go well with you and that you may enjoy long life on the earth."

EPHESIANS 6:2–3 NIV

At the sound of the quirky strains of "Take Me Out to the Ball Game"—the distinctive ring on his cell phone—Steve rolled over in bed and glanced at the clock. Eight-thirty in the morning. Who could be calling at this hour? Groggily, he reached for the phone as "root, root, root for the home team" finished playing; voice mail must have picked up the call before he got to it, which was fine with him. He needed to sleep at least another hour before he could talk to anyone.

When he finally woke up, Steve checked his voice mail. Sure enough, it was another phone call from home. If it wasn't his mother, it was his father or one of the twins, his thirteen-year-old brother and sister. Theirs had always been a loving and close-knit family, but Steve had talked to them more since he moved away than he had when he was living with them. He didn't want to hurt them. He just needed some breathing space.

It's hard on everyone when one member of the family leaves home, but it's especially hard when those left behind won't let go. Maybe that's the situation you face now that you've graduated. You're excited about your new life, but you're finding it hard to enjoy your independence. How can you tell your family that it's time to let you go without hurting them?

Try approaching them with some practical ideas on how you can stay in touch—but first, go to God and talk it over with Him. He has a storehouse of practical solutions to whatever problems you face. Even better, He can prepare your parents' hearts and give you the words that will best convey to them both your love and your need for independence.

Steve did just that: He prayed about the situation throughout the week and wrote down whatever impressions came to his mind. By the end of the week, he was startled by everything God had shown him. For one thing he realized that what bothered him the most was the *timing* of the calls. With mostly afternoon classes and a late-night job at a twenty-four-hour coffee shop on campus, he resented the morning phone calls, but he had never adequately explained his schedule to his family. The revelations continued, and eventually Steve and his family worked out a system that allowed them to keep in touch and allowed Steve his freedom as well.

There are lots of ways that you can stay in touch with your

family without feeling as if they are encroaching on your independence. Take the initiative. Let your family in on your new life in ways that work for everyone. Most important, let them know that your love for them survived your move away from them.

Your family situation may be radically different from Steve's. No matter what the circumstances, once you leave home, even temporarily, your parents and siblings will face a void in their lives. If you don't take the initiative to stay in touch with them, they will be left wondering how you are, what you are doing, what your new life is like—and of course, whether you're eating right and dressing warmly enough.

Ask God for creative ways to keep them informed about your life. The more you do on your end, the less need they will have to keep calling. For a change call them once in a while. Send an occasional postcard or note. Surprise them with an unexpected weekend visit. Send them clippings about things that are of interest to them. If you're in the military, find similar ways to stay in touch.

If your family is Internet savvy, take maximum advantage of that medium. Set up your own Web page that you update periodically; that's a great way for them to get a glimpse of your life while you're away. Begin a private list for family members so that everyone keeps informed. E-mail them regularly, and set up times when every member of your family can meet in a private chat room for an online conversation.

I Will

Seek God's creative solutions for staying in touch with my family.

yes _____ no _____

Understand the void that my leaving has created in their lives.

yes _____ no _____

Take the initiative in communicating with those back home.

yes _____ no _____

Realize that I need to trust God to give my family the grace to let go.

yes _____ no _____

Keep my family informed about what is going on in my life.

yes _____ no _____

Things to Do

☐ Decide how often you feel it's appropriate to call home—once a week, once every two weeks—and post a reminder so you can be the one to call them.

☐ If you don't have a cell phone with free long distance, buy a phone card to keep costs down.

☐ Spend your prayer time over the next week focusing on your family. Write down the impressions God gives you.

☐ Get a friend to take photos of you in your new environment and send them to your family.

☐ Spend some time throughout the week "talking" to your family using a tape recorder. When the tape is full, send it to them.

Things to Remember

Those who bring trouble on their families will have nothing at the end. Foolish people will always be servants to the wise.

PROVERBS 11:29 GNT

[God said,] "All of you must have respect for your mother and father. You must always keep my Sabbath days: I am the LORD your God."

LEVITICUS 19:3 NIrV

How good and pleasant it is when brothers live together in unity!
Psalm 133:1 NIV

May the God who gives endurance and encouragement give you a spirit of unity among yourselves as you follow Christ Jesus.

ROMANS 15:5 NIV

Put up with hard times. God uses them to train you. He is treating you as children. What children are not trained by their parents?

HEBREWS 12:7 NIrV

Keep your father's command, and do not forsake the law of your mother.

PROVERBS 6:20 NKJV

Even if my father and mother abandon me, the LORD will hold me close.

PSALM 27:10 NLT

Those who curse their father or mother will be like a light going out in darkness.

PROVERBS 20:20 NCV

If any do not take care of their relatives, especially the members of their own family, they have denied the faith and are worse than an unbeliever.

1 TIMOTHY 5:8 GNT

Raging water cannot extinguish love, and rivers will never wash it away. If a man exchanged all his family's wealth for love, people would utterly despise him.

SONG OF SOLOMON 8:7 GOD'S WORD

My son, listen. Accept what I say. Then you will live for many years.

PROVERBS 4:10 NIrV

Other things may change us, but we start and end with family.

ANTHONY BRANDT

A family is a place where principles are hammered and honed on the anvil of everyday living.

CHARLES SWINDOLL

Ethics

Who's to Know?

Let integrity and uprightness preserve me, for I wait for You.

PSALM 25:21 NKJV

Remember the baseball team in New York that lost its Little League World Series title in 2001? The team's standout pitcher was too old for Little League, and from all indications, the coach was well aware of it. Look around in your own community: Have any of the schools reportedly fudged a bit on the way they administer standardized tests? Has a local employee been caught with her hand in the company's "cookie jar"—the cash account used for incidental expenses? How about the local university? Didn't you read somewhere that the athletics department may have violated its own recruitment policy? It's apparent that ethical problems plague all levels of American society.

Those kinds of ethical dilemmas represent only the tip of the iceberg, however. In your day-to-day life, you face a host of ethical decisions that may not be as visible or newsworthy as those described above, but they are no less important. That's because ethical decisions build on each other: Every time you choose to do right, you make it much easier to choose to do right the next time.

Conversely, every decision to do the wrong thing makes it easier to do the wrong thing next time.

You already own the most comprehensive text ever published on ethics, and you don't have to go to college to understand it. It's the Bible, of course. Its pages contain the moral code you need to live by in order to be in right relation with God and with others. God's principles of right and wrong conduct supersede all others, and He wants those principles to become an integral part of your character. Then, when you're faced with an ethical dilemma, you can immediately focus on the biblical principle rather than the details—which often confuse the issue. For example, if you understand the principle that cheating is wrong, then there's no way you would even consider your roommate's latest scheme for acquiring the answers to next week's history exam. You already know the right thing to do.

Saturate your mind and your spirit with what the Bible has to say about right and wrong. Be aware of the ethical lessons found on nearly every page. Most important, learn those lessons so well that the underlying biblical principles become a guiding force in your life. God provided those principles for your benefit, so you can maintain a clear conscience and right standing with Him and with other people.

I Will

Realize that ethical decisions build on each other. _____yes_____ _____no_____

Rely on the Bible as the ultimate textbook on ethics. _____yes_____ _____no_____

Trust God to help me face the many ethical challenges in my daily life. _____yes_____ _____no_____

Learn from the biblical lessons on right and wrong. _____yes_____ _____no_____

Resolve to do the right thing, even when no one else does. _____yes_____ _____no_____

Be thankful for God's forgiveness for the times I've blown it in the past. _____yes_____ _____no_____

Things to Do

☐ Familiarize yourself with current ethical problems presented in a Christian magazine article, either in print or online (such as www.christianitytoday.com).

☐ Promise God and yourself that you will be scrupulously honest when filling out applications, creating a résumé, and filing your taxes.

☐ Ask God to increase your sensitivity to the ethical dilemmas you are facing.

☐ Read about the problems in the church at Corinth and the method Paul used to deal with them.

☐ Keep ethics in mind the next time you read, hear, or watch the news.

Things to Remember

Lord, who may abide in Your tabernacle? Who may dwell in Your holy hill? He who walks uprightly, and works righteousness, and speaks the truth in his heart.

PSALM 15:1–2 NKJV

If we had forgotten the name of our God, or extended our hands to a strange god; would not God find this out? For He knows the secrets of the heart.

PSALM 44:20–21 NASB

They show that in their hearts they know what is right and wrong, just as the law commands. And they show this by their consciences. Sometimes their thoughts tell them they did wrong, and sometimes their thoughts tell them they did right.

ROMANS 2:15 NCV

Create in me a clean heart, O God, and renew a steadfast spirit within me.

PSALM 51:10 NKJV

Lord, you have examined me and know all about me. You know when I sit down and when I get up. You know my thoughts before I think them.

PSALM 139:1–2 NCV

Evangelical faith without Christian ethics is a travesty on the gospel.

V. RAYMOND EDMAN

Ethics and equity and the principles of justice do not change with the calendar.

D. H. LAWRENCE

Failure

Your Life's Greatest Work

My flesh and my heart fail; but God is the strength of my heart and my portion forever.

PSALM 73:26 NKJV

Glenn Holland was distraught. His carefully designed plan to dedicate his life to composing symphonies fell apart when he discovered that his wife was pregnant. He was forced to keep working as a high school music teacher, and he had no time to create great symphonies and become the world-renowned composer he had envisioned. This story, of course, is a synopsis of the 1995 movie *Mr. Holland's Opus,* and it's a masterful look at one man's skewed understanding of what success really is. All he can see, it seems, are his many failures, while all along success is staring him in the face.

Holland's idea of failure was self-imposed. The world can also make a person feel like a failure. What matters, though, is God's view of failure and success—and that very often may run counter to what the world and you think. God can take your most dismal failures and turn them into such remarkable successes that you're likely to end up wondering how on earth He did it.

Understand first and foremost that as one who has been created in the image of God, you are not a failure. Remember, too, that God's promises have never failed, and He has promised you all kinds of good things in this life and the next as long as your heart is turned toward Him. One of those good things is success, but like many other concepts, success is in the eye of the beholder—and when the beholder is God, well, its appearance may be radically different from what the world sees. In His eyes, loving Him and serving other people are enough to make you wildly successful.

Everyone's life is filled with failure—big and little, public and private, inconsequential and highly significant. What separates genuinely successful people from the rest of the pack is their attitude toward failure. Each time they fail, they pick themselves up, dust off their failure, and get back to work. You have a distinct advantage: Every time you fail, you can call on the Father to lift you up and walk with you as you head back to the task at hand.

Trust God to help you overcome your failures, and learn to see genuine success for what it is—a life lived in the will of God, in accordance with His principles, and in service to others. Then your opus—your life's greatest work—will be a guaranteed success in the eyes of the One who matters most.

I Will

Understand that true success involves loving God
and serving others.   _yes_   _no_

Stop measuring success by the world's standards.   _yes_   _no_

Trust God to pick me up when I've failed.   _yes_   _no_

Learn from my mistakes.   _yes_   _no_

Believe that God can turn my dismal failures into
remarkable successes.   _yes_   _no_

Realize that everyone fails at times.   _yes_   _no_

Never give up; keep on working.   _yes_   _no_

Things to Do

☐ Write out a definition of success from a biblical perspective.

☐ Read about the personal and professional failings of a nineteenth-century man named James Pierpont—and the "opus" of his life.

☐ Make a list of the things you believe you've failed at and write down what your successes from those same efforts were.

☐ Watch Mr. Holland's Opus in light of the concepts of failure and success.

☐ Pray Psalm 73 back to God.

☐ Decide what you need to change to be a success in what you are doing in your life right now.

☐ Ask God to show you His path to success in your future.

Things to Remember

Not one of all the LORD's good promises to the house of Israel failed; every one was fulfilled.

JOSHUA 21:45 NIV

The LORD will make you the head, not the tail. You will always be at the top, never at the bottom, if you faithfully obey the commands of the LORD your God that I am giving you today.

DEUTERONOMY 28:13 GOD'S WORD

A good person will never fail; he will always be remembered.

PSALM 112:6 GNT

Get all the advice you can, and you will succeed; without it you will fail.

PROVERBS 15:22 GNT

Let us try as hard as we can to enter God's rest so that no one will fail by following the example of those who refused to obey.

HEBREWS 4:11 NCV

Failure is success if we learn from it.

MALCOLM S. FORBES

A man can get discouraged many times but he is not a failure until he begins to blame somebody else and stops trying.

JOHN BURROUGHS

Mastering Money

A good person leaves what he owns to his children and grandchildren. But a sinner's wealth is stored up for those who do right.

—PROVERBS 13:22 NIrV

Whether you are just starting out in a new career or have years of college or military service before you join the workforce full time, it's never too early to start making critical decisions about how you will give, save, and spend your income. Money problems can create havoc in your future marriage and family, chain you to a job you are ill-suited for, interfere with your relationships with God and other people, and hinder your service to God and others. Money is not a commodity to take lightly. From God's perspective, money is a means of providing for your needs and the needs of others.

As you embark on your new postgraduation life, you would be wise to create a budget—or as some prefer to call it, a spending plan. The word *budget* can sound like a punishment, whereas a "spending plan" carries the idea that you are in control of where your money goes. The important principle here is that you control your money; your money does not control you.

How do you, as a believer in God, create a workable spending plan, especially since your income may be uncertain and will fluctuate throughout your lifetime? You begin to think in percentages instead of dollar amounts. Ten percent will always be 10 percent, regardless of how much or how little you make.

And 10 percent is where you need to start, by making an irreversible decision to return at least one-tenth of your income—a tithe—to God, who has given you everything you have to begin with. No other money decision you make will be as critical as this one, because the decision to tithe has eternal consequences. The money you give to God helps spread the Good News to others, opening to them the possibility of a new life in Christ and an eternal life with God. God promises to bless you when you tithe, but your motivation should always be obedience to Him and a desire to support the work of the church, not personal gain.

What you decide next can make a significant difference in the quality of your financial life in the future. Many Christians skip straight from tithing to spending, ignoring what should be the second step—saving. The earlier you get in the habit of saving, the better. When you are young and your expenses are far less than they will be when you have a family, you may be able to put 10 to 20 percent of your income in savings. Look into short-term savings and long-term investment accounts rather than thinking only in terms of a savings account at a bank.

Spending can be a challenge for a new graduate. For the first time in your life, you may be making "real" money, and the temptation will be there to spend money on things you could never afford before. Restrain yourself. Learn to be a disciplined consumer. Watch out for the constant lure of more and bigger and better. Become aware of the techniques advertisers use to get you to buy the products they are pitching. Slogans like "You deserve it" and "You've earned it" and "Do yourself a favor" subtly play on your psyche; you start to think, *I do deserve it, I have earned it, and I am going to do myself a favor.* Do yourself a real favor: Ignore the marketers.

Finally, stay out of debt. You've probably been inundated with credit card offers; finance companies consider graduates to be some of their best prospects. Recent graduates see their future income as set in stone; why not get what they want and need now by charging their purchases and paying them off with their future paychecks? That's the way credit card companies are hoping you'll start to think. They know your income is not guaranteed and you cannot predict your future expenses. Meanwhile, interest charges keep increasing, and you get further in debt. Learn to live on what you have, not what you hope you'll have.

You cannot place your trust in wealth; you cannot place your confidence in the prospect of a steady paycheck; you cannot control the future, with its emergencies and unexpected expenses and economic uncertainties. You can control the way you handle your money. Learn to look at money from God's perspective, and seek His wisdom in handling it.

I Will

Understand that my security comes from God alone. _yes_ _no_

Realize that I can control my money rather than
allow it to control me. _yes_ _no_

Seek God's wisdom in handling my finances. _yes_ _no_

Make sure my motivation in giving is a godly one. _yes_ _no_

Realize that God has given me everything I have. _yes_ _no_

Entrust my future income and expenses into
God's hands. _yes_ _no_

Things to Do

☐ *Create a workable spending plan, no matter what your current
income is.*

☐ *Make an irreversible decision to tithe.*

☐ *Open a savings account or, if you already have one, try to find one
with a higher yield.*

☐ *Find a ministry or missions project that you would like to
help support.*

☐ *Ask God to give you wisdom in your money-related decisions.*

☐ *Read what the Bible says about money, using an online or other
concordance.*

Things to Remember

[Jesus said,] "The master answered, 'You did well. You are a good and loyal servant. Because you were loyal with small things, I will let you care for much greater things. Come and share my joy with me.' "

MATTHEW 25:23 NCV

"Bring the whole tithe into the storehouse, so that there may be food in My house, and test Me now in this," says the LORD of hosts, "if I will not open for you the windows of heaven and pour out for you a blessing until it overflows."

MALACHI 3:10 NASB

Dishonest money dwindles away, but he who gathers money little by little makes it grow.
Proverbs 13:11 NIV

Whoever loves money will never be satisfied with money. Whoever loves wealth will never be satisfied with more income. Even this is pointless.

ECCLESIASTES 5:10 GOD'S WORD

My God will meet all your needs according to his glorious riches in Christ Jesus.

PHILIPPIANS 4:19 NIV

[God says,] "Come, all you who are thirsty, come to the waters; and you who have no money, come, buy and eat! Come, buy wine and milk without money and without cost."

ISAIAH 55:1 NIV

The love of money is at the root of all kinds of evil. And some people, craving money, have wandered from the faith and pierced themselves with many sorrows.

1 TIMOTHY 6:10 NLT

[Jesus said,] "No one can serve two masters. Either he will hate the one and love the other, or he will be devoted to the one and despise the other. You cannot serve both God and Money."

MATTHEW 6:24 NIV

Keep your lives free from the love of money, and be content with what you have; for he has said, "I will never leave you or forsake you."

HEBREWS 13:5 NRSV

[God says,] "Why do you spend money for what is not bread, and your wages for what does not satisfy? Listen carefully to Me, and eat what is good, and delight yourself in abundance."

ISAIAH 55:2 NASB

Money makes a good servant, but a bad master.

FRANCIS BACON

Money cannot buy peace of mind. It cannot heal ruptured relationships, or build meaning into a life that has none.

RICHARD DeVos

Moving Mountains

Some trust in chariots, and some in horses; but we will remember the name of the Lord our God.

Psalm 20:7 NKJV

"I just don't have enough faith for that." Have you heard someone say words to that effect? Maybe it was a friend or a relative—or maybe it was you. For whatever reason, when some Christians find themselves in a hard place, they often have a hard time remembering Jesus' words about faith in Matthew 17. Speaking to His disciples, He said that even a tiny measure of faith—as small as a mustard seed—is enough to move mountains.

How big is a mustard seed? A mustard seed is only ¹⁄₁₆ of an inch. It would take at least sixteen of them lined up to equal just one inch. If you are a believer, you can surely muster up that much faith.

Your faith begins to erode the moment you take your eyes off God and start looking at the results of your faith. You command a mountain to move, and you can't even get a pebble to budge. *That's it,* you think. *I just don't have enough faith.* What exactly is faith? It's believing that God is who He says He is, that He is capable of doing all that He says He is capable of doing, and that He will do for you exactly what He says He will do for you. Faith involves not only believing all that with your head, but also trusting all that with your heart.

What's the problem? Why can't you move that mountain? Maybe you're looking at the wrong mountain; the one behind you just crumbled to the sea, but you're stubbornly looking at the one straight ahead. Maybe you haven't waited long enough, or maybe God wants you to plant your mustard-seed faith somewhere else. Remember, it's not faith if trust is not at work, and genuine trust is not something that you would abandon at the first hint that maybe God has decided not to come through for you after all. Genuine trust hangs in there, believing that God's timing and God's ways of answering prayer are often very different from what you were expecting.

Hebrews 11:1 reminds you that faith is the confident assurance that what you hope for is going to happen and the evidence of things you cannot yet see. God wants you to continue to walk in that confident assurance and believe in the reality of that unseen evidence. To do that, you need to take God at His word. You need to always remember that your faith is in Him—not in the amount of faith you have.

I Will

Guard against the possible erosion of my faith. _yes_ _no_

Take my questions directly to God. _yes_ _no_

Protect whatever measure of faith I have. _yes_ _no_

Believe that God will do what He says He will do. _yes_ _no_

Learn to rely on God's timing and God's ways instead of my own. _yes_ _no_

Trust God to increase the measure of faith I have. _yes_ _no_

Be sensitive to just what it is God wants me to pray for. _yes_ _no_

Things to Do

☐ *Read what Jesus had to say in Matthew 17:14–23 after His disciples failed to drive out a demon.*

☐ *Meditate on what Jesus meant when He said you could move mountains.*

☐ *Find a buddy, another strong Christian, who will help keep you strong in your faith.*

☐ *Use an online Bible search to find out what the Bible says about faith.*

☐ *Ask God to give you the strength to protect your faith.*

☐ *Read Hebrews 11, often called "God's Hall of Fame" because of its description of people of faith.*

Things to Remember

We live by faith, not by sight.

2 CORINTHIANS 5:7 NIV

At all times carry faith as a shield; for with it you will be able to put out all the burning arrows shot by the Evil One.

EPHESIANS 6:16 GNT

Listen, my beloved brethren: Has God not chosen the poor of this world to be rich in faith and heirs of the kingdom which He promised to those who love Him?

JAMES 2:5 NKJV

What is faith? It is the confident assurance that what we hope for is going to happen. It is the evidence of things we cannot yet see.

HEBREWS 11:1 NLT

The righteousness of God is revealed from faith to faith; as it is written, "The just shall live by faith."

ROMANS 1:17 NKJV

Obedience is the fruit of faith.

CHRISTINA ROSSETTI

Faith is to believe what we do not see; and the reward of this faith is to see what we believe.

SAINT AUGUSTINE

Fear

Facing the Unknown

There is no fear in love; but perfect love casts out fear, because fear involves torment. But he who fears has not been made perfect in love.

1 JOHN 4:18 NKJV

Alex woke up with a start. Something about this day was different . . . what was it? Ah, yes. As his brain kicked in to gear, he remembered: Today really was the first day of the rest of his life. Yesterday—graduation day—had been so full of activities that he had managed to forget the fear that had tormented him over the last few weeks. His fears were so many that he had lost count, but he remembered the biggies, like the fear of moving to Manhattan to attend Columbia and even the fear of attending Columbia itself—or any other university for that matter—but mostly, the fear that he just wouldn't be able to hack it, no matter where he went or what he did.

What Alex really feared was the future. That's understandable for a newly graduated young man or woman. Maybe you've experienced that same kind of fear, and you've started wondering, with some trepidation, what's up ahead. What will the future hold for you—success or failure, happiness or misery, love or loneliness? The future can indeed appear frightening. God does not want you to live in fear, and He wants you to be excited about the future He has in store for you.

How do you get over this fear of the unknown future that awaits you? Ask God to release you from the stranglehold that fear has on your life and replace it with the spirit of "power, love, and self-discipline" that He promises in 2 Timothy 1:7 (NLT). He holds your future in His hands, and you can trust Him with it. What's more, He loves you with a perfect love and wants only the best for you. John writes that God's perfect love actually "casts out fear"—it flings fear away and removes the torment that plagues you when you're frightened. Imagine God taking your fear away from you and throwing it where it will never be found again. That's a powerful image you can carry with you throughout your life.

When you come to understand the depth of love that God has for you, you can face your future with confidence. Place a high priority on understanding and experiencing His love. As you walk in the light of that love, you will realize that there's no room for fear in the kind of trusting and loving relationship God wants to have with you.

I Will

Entrust my future to God.   _yes_   _no_

Walk in the light of God's love.   _yes_   _no_

Believe the biblical promises regarding fear.   _yes_   _no_

Cultivate a trusting and loving relationship
with God.   _yes_   _no_

Learn to face the coming years with excitement
and confidence.   _yes_   _no_

Trust that God wants the best for me.   _yes_   _no_

Have confidence that God will give me a spirit of
power, love, and self-discipline.   _yes_   _no_

Things to Do

☐ Memorize Psalm 27:1 or Hebrews 13:6. Or better yet, both.

☐ Buy a "promise book," an inexpensive book that sorts the promises in
   the Bible into different categories, such as fear, love, and eternal life.

☐ Make a list of the specific things you fear right now. Pray about each
   item on the list, then tear it up and throw it away.

☐ Write "Perfect love casts out fear" on an index card and display it in a
   prominent place in your room.

☐ Ask God to release the grip that fear has on your life.

☐ Give God your fear of the future and imagine Him casting it away.

Things to Remember

The LORD is my light and my salvation; whom shall I fear? The LORD is the strength of my life; of whom shall I be afraid?

PSALM 27:1 NKJV

Don't be bluffed into silence by the threats of bullies. There's nothing they can do to your soul, your core being. Save your fear for God, who holds your entire life—body and soul—in his hands.

MATTHEW 10:28 THE MESSAGE

[Jesus] said to them, "Why are you so fearful? How is it that you have no faith?"

MARK 4:40 NKJV

We say with confidence, "The Lord is my helper; I will not be afraid. What can man do to me?"

HEBREWS 13:6 NIV

God has not given us a spirit of fear and timidity, but of power, love, and self-discipline.

2 TIMOTHY 1:7 NLT

The worst sorrows in life are not in its losses and misfortune, but its fears.

ARTHUR CHRISTOPHER BENSON

Comfort zones are plush, lined coffins. When you stay in your plush, lined coffins, you die.

STAN DALE

Responsibility

Following Through

Arise, for this matter is your responsibility. We also are with you. Be of good courage, and do it.

EZRA 10:4 NKJV

The competition for a summer internship in Washington was heating up. All of Professor Strickland's political science students knew where they stood in the competition, and they didn't stand a chance against the two top contenders, Luke and Vanessa. Both worked as student aides in the poli-sci department and excelled academically. Both had written brilliant essays on how they intended to make the most of the internship.

On paper Luke had a slight edge, and the rest of the students figured it was enough to clinch the position in Washington for him. He had a 4.4 grade point average to Vanessa's 4.1; he had aced every one of Strickland's exams; and his father had been a two-term U.S. Senator when Luke was younger. From his father he knew details about how the government *really* worked.

It caught just about everyone by surprise when Strickland granted the internship to Vanessa. Luke was stunned. He made an appointment to see the professor.

"Sir, I don't understand," he said and began listing his credentials. "Luke, your academic credentials are impeccable," Strickland said. "There's more to this than grades. While you were working so hard trying to outdo Vanessa's GPA, she was picking up your responsibilities in the department, the ones you thought were less important than your grades."

People who are in positions of responsibility—the people who will make decisions that affect your future—place a high value on finding that quality in others. They look for a person who diligently performs the duties assigned to her and meets whatever obligations she has. They look for a person who knows what is expected of him and follows through on it. They look for people who know how important it is to keep the commitments they make.

Not surprisingly, God also places a high value on the quality of responsibility. He wants all of His people to act responsibly in every area of their lives, but especially with regard to their spiritual lives.

So—how do you rate yourself? Do you consider yourself to be a responsible person? Maybe you are responsible in some areas of your life but not others; for instance, you may be like Luke, who was responsible academically but faltered when it came to his other obligations.

Take a look at your spiritual life. In regard to your relationship with God, you know what is expected of you— love Him, serve Him, obey Him, worship Him. Without placing an unrealistically high standard on yourself, can you say you handle your relationship with Him responsibly? What about your service to others? Lots of young people sign up to help out with ministries in the church, but their other obligations often get in the way. How about you? Do you follow through and do what you say you will do?

Then there's your primary endeavor at this point in your life. That may be college or graduate school, a full-time job, or military service. All three areas carry certain duties and obligations. How would you say your performance of those duties and obligations stacks up against the performance standards established by the school, the workplace, or the armed services?

Finally, you have social responsibilities, to your family, your friends, your neighbors, and others. Do you make commitments to those people and keep them? Those commitments cover a wide range of activities, everything from promising to visit your grandmother in the nursing home to cutting your neighbor's grass to following through on your weekend plans with a friend—even if you just got a better offer. How you meet your social responsibilities is every bit as important as the way you meet your other obligations, because it reveals important truths about your character.

In every area of your life, God wants you to act responsibly. He gave you a conscience for a purpose, and part of that purpose was to serve as a reminder that you should always do what is expected of you, to the best of your abilities. Following through on your commitments is a certain sign of maturity, one that will be sure to attract the attention of those people who are in a position to affect your future.

I Will

Understand that God wants me to act responsibly in every area of my life.

yes _____ *no* _____

Follow through on what is expected of me.

yes _____ *no* _____

Keep the commitments I make.

yes _____ *no* _____

Look to God to activate my conscience when I am tempted to renege on an obligation.

yes _____ *no* _____

Recognize a sense of responsibility as an essential characteristic of maturity.

yes _____ *no* _____

Trust God to give me the strength to handle all of my responsibilities.

yes _____ *no* _____

Things to Do

☐ *List your commitments and decide if you are following through on them responsibly.*

☐ *Ask God to reveal those areas in which your sense of responsibility may be faltering.*

☐ *Decide how you can improve your performance, based on what God reveals to you.*

☐ *In your journal describe the way you see the relationship between responsibility and maturity.*

☐ *Read one of the parables of Jesus that deals with responsible behavior (for example, the Faithful Servant in Luke 12:42–48 or the Ten Minas in Luke 19:11–27).*

Things to Remember

We then who are strong ought to bear with the scruples of the weak, and not to please ourselves. Let each of us please his neighbor for his good, leading to edification.

ROMANS 15:1–2 NKJV

Now all has been heard; here is the conclusion of the matter: Fear God and keep his commandments, for this is the whole duty of man.

ECCLESIASTES 12:13 NIV

Paul looked straight at the Sanhedrin and said, "My brothers, I have fulfilled my duty to God in all good conscience to this day."

ACTS 23:1 NIV

I have written you quite boldly on some points, as if to remind you of them again, because of the grace God gave me to be a minister of Christ Jesus to the Gentiles with the priestly duty of proclaiming the gospel of God, so that the Gentiles might become an offering acceptable to God, sanctified by the Holy Spirit.

ROMANS 15:15–16 NIV

Till we all come to the unity of the faith and of the knowledge of the Son of God, to a perfect man, to the measure of the stature of the fullness of Christ; that we should no longer be children, tossed to and fro and carried about with every wind of doctrine, by the trickery of men, in the cunning craftiness of deceitful plotting.

EPHESIANS 4:13–14 NKJV

If a man makes a vow to the LORD, or takes an oath to bind himself with a binding obligation, he shall not violate his word; he shall do according to all that proceeds out of his mouth.

NUMBERS 30:2 NASB

Perseverance must finish its work so that you may be mature and complete, not lacking anything.

JAMES 1:4 NIV

[David said to Solomon,] "I'm about to leave this world. Be strong and mature. Fulfill your duty to the LORD your God. Obey his directions, laws, commands, rules, and written instructions as they are recorded in Moses' Teachings. Then you'll succeed in everything you do wherever you may go."

1 KINGS 2:2–3 GOD'S WORD

[Paul wrote,] However, we do use wisdom to speak to those who are mature. It is a wisdom that doesn't belong to this world or to the rulers of this world who are in power today and gone tomorrow.

1 CORINTHIANS 2:6 GOD'S WORD

In the last analysis, the individual person is responsible for living his own life and for "finding himself." If he persists in shifting his responsibility to somebody else, he fails to find out the meaning of his own existence.

THOMAS MERTON

It is not only what we do, but also what we do not do for which we are accountable.

MOLIÈRE

Fellowship

In One Accord

That which we have seen and heard we declare to you, that you also may have fellowship with us; and truly our fellowship is with the Father and with His Son Jesus Christ.

1 JOHN 1:3 NKJV

Fellowship is one of the hallmarks of the Christian faith. In fact Jesus and the writers of the epistles emphasized fellowship—the bond you share with your fellow brothers and sisters in Christ—far more than they did friendship, which you can have even with nonbelievers as long as you manage those relationships carefully. You can have genuine fellowship, however, only with other believers.

Why does the New Testament place so much emphasis on fellowship? Isn't it important to have one or two close friendships with Christians whom you trust with the private details of your life? Of course. You should always seek out like-minded, trustworthy, believing friends. But you must also take care to seek the fellowship of larger groups of believers, not only so you'll have others with whom to share aspects of your spiritual life (like worship), but also because the Lord intends for His followers to look out for each other and take care of each other in practical ways (like providing meals, transportation, and emotional support during a crisis).

Graduation marks a time when you will be uprooted, even if you continue to live at home for a while. If you're staying home, your church youth group may no longer feel like a place where you belong. If you're leaving home for college or the military, you'll be leaving behind whatever fellowship you once had. Finding other believers with whom you can fellowship in your new environment—or an older age group—will make the postgraduation transition far smoother than you may realize. It's something that's all too easy to put off but that will make a critical difference in your spiritual life. True fellowship forms a blanket of protection, comfort, and love around you—not a bad thing to have when you're suddenly faced with the unfamiliar to the max.

Keep in mind another crucial difference between friendship and fellowship: You pretty much have to like your friends or else they wouldn't be friends, but you do not have to like the brothers and sisters in Christ with whom you fellowship. You just have to love them. There will always be believers in your life who get on your nerves or act weird or may not like you (and show it). Accept that fact, and get back to the business of showing the world what genuine Christian love is, through the bond of fellowship that knits believers together.

I Will

Appreciate the distinctive understanding of
fellowship in a Christian context.

yes _no_

Actively seek out Christian fellowship in my new
(or old) environment.

yes _no_

Recognize both the spiritual and practical benefits
of fellowship.

yes _no_

See Christian fellowship as a means of showing the
world an example of God's love.

yes _no_

Learn to love believers that I don't necessarily like.

yes _no_

Encourage others to remain in fellowship when
I see them backing away.

yes _no_

Things to Do

☐ Ask other Christians for their help in finding a group you can
fellowship with.

☐ Read the book of 1 John and notice its emphasis on love among
Christians.

☐ Pray Psalm 133 back to God.

☐ Think of a practical way you can help a fellow believer (not a friend)
and do it.

☐ Meditate on the concept of fellowship as the Big Miracle of Love, as
Jess Moody describes it in the quotation that follows.

☐ Keep a notebook handy in which you can write down the prayer needs
of fellow believers (and pray about them).

Things to Remember

[John wrote to the Christian congregations,] We announce to you what we have seen and heard, because we want you also to have fellowship with us. Our fellowship is with God the Father and with his Son, Jesus Christ.

1 JOHN 1:3 NCV

[Paul wrote of the Colossians and other believers,] My goal is that they will be encouraged and knit together by strong ties of love. I want them to have full confidence because they have complete understanding of God's secret plan, which is Christ himself.

COLOSSIANS 2:2 NLT

We [David and his friends] had intimate talks with each other and worshiped together in the Temple.

PSALM 55:14 GNT

Those who had respect for the LORD talked with one another. They cheered each other up. And the LORD heard them. A list of people and what they did was written on a scroll in front of him. It included the names of those who respected the LORD and honored him.

MALACHI 3:16 NIrV

We will win the world when we realize that fellowship, not evangelism, must be our primary emphasis. When we demonstrate the Big Miracle of Love, it won't be necessary for us to go out—they will come in.

JESS MOODY

Many men do not understand that the need for fellowship is really as deep as the need for food, and so they go through life accepting many substitutes for genuine, warm, simple fellowship.

JOSHUA LOTH LIEBMAN

Flexibility

A Change in the Program

[Jesus] told them this parable: "No one tears a patch from a new garment and sews it on an old one. If he does, he will have torn the new garment, and the patch from the new will not match the old."

LUKE 5:36 NIV

No matter what your plans are after graduation, God is doing a new thing in your life. That may sound exciting, and it is. As you branch out and begin to explore the world around you on an entirely different level, you will encounter new ideas and opportunities, and you can be sure that when you do, you will sometimes need to adjust your thinking. As long as you make those adjustments in response to God's leading, you can be confident that these "new things" will not lead you to do anything contrary to His word.

Unless you remain flexible, you run the risk of becoming a modern-day Pharisee. Among the many offenses the Pharisees chastised Jesus and His followers for was their habit of upsetting the old way of doing things. One such offense was introducing new and radical concepts, like sharing a meal with—horrors!—a tax collector and other assorted sinful people. The disciples themselves were not immune to inflexible religious thinking. It took a vision and some strong words from God for Peter to realize that the gospel was available to Gentiles as well as to Jews. More subtle but just as rigid is the way a contemporary church or other group of believers can start out with an open and accommodating approach to faith but end up with a rigid "my way or the highway" attitude.

Being flexible does not mean that you should ever lower your standards or alter your beliefs in a way that would conflict with biblical truth. Jesus taught His disciples to be flexible primarily when it came to dealing with other people. "Make allowances for each person's unique place in his or her relationship to God," He seemed to say through His words as well as His actions. "Be prepared to see Me change the program on you in order to do a new thing that you may not understand completely."

That's good advice for you today. Some of your most cherished opinions may evaporate when confronted by an unfamiliar but logical argument that still lines up with the truth of Scripture. Some of the believers you meet are likely to come from denominations whose worship styles differ from yours. Some of the people God places in your path may not be at all the kind of people you thought He would want you to associate with. God is stretching you; your responsibility is to remain pliable and elastic in His hands.

I Will

Obey God even when I don't completely understand
the changes He's making.

_____ yes   _____ no

Remain flexible in the hands of God.

_____ yes   _____ no

Be aware of those areas in which I am likely to
become rigid and resistant to God's leading.

_____ yes   _____ no

Accept other believers who may be at a different
level of maturity than I am.

_____ yes   _____ no

Understand that opinions can change and still line
up with Scripture.

_____ yes   _____ no

Realize that God will never lead me to do anything
contrary to His word.

_____ yes   _____ no

Things to Do

☐ To understand flexibility, read the story of Cornelius and Peter in Acts
10, in which God revamped Peter's religiously programmed thinking.

☐ Attend a service at a church whose customs are unfamiliar to you (it's
best if you can go with someone who knows the routine).

☐ Choose one of your most strongly held opinions and write out an
argument for the opposite viewpoint.

☐ Make a list of the things that could be keeping you from being more
open to new things, such as pride or fear.

☐ Ask God to remove from your life anything that serves as an obstacle
to change.

Things to Remember

So then, let us stop judging one another. Instead you should decide never to do anything that would make others stumble or fall into sin.

ROMANS 14:13 GNT

Be humble and gentle. Be patient with each other, making allowance for each other's faults because of your love.

EPHESIANS 4:2 NLT

Receive one who is weak in the faith, but not to disputes over doubtful things.

ROMANS 14:1 NKJV

You must make allowance for each other's faults and forgive the person who offends you. Remember, the Lord forgave you, so you must forgive others.

COLOSSIANS 3:13 NLT

One person esteems one day above another; another esteems every day alike. Let each be fully convinced in his own mind.

ROMANS 14:5 NKJV

Behold, I will do a new thing, now it shall spring forth; shall you not know it? I will even make a road in the wilderness and rivers in the desert.

ISAIAH 43:19 NKJV

We are all bound to the throne of the Supreme Being by a flexible chain which restrains without enslaving us. The most wonderful aspect of the universal scheme of things is the action of free beings under divine guidance.

JOSEPH DE MAISTRE

We are free to yield to truth.

HORACE

Loneliness

Is Anyone There?

Turn to me and be gracious to me, for I am lonely and afflicted.

PSALM 25:16 NIV

Sitting in Starbucks with five of her friends, Amy realized she hadn't heard a word anyone had said for the past few minutes. As she tuned back in and tried to pick up on the conversation, she discovered that she didn't have a clue what they were talking about. This kind of thing had been happening far too often lately; her mind would wander off and she would feel empty and alone, even when she was surrounded by her friends.

That's what baffled her the most: How could she feel so lonely when she shared an apartment with three other girls, spent lots of time with her steady boyfriend, and worked in a busy department store in the middle of a reasonably large city? She couldn't even attribute the problem to homesickness, because she spoke to her family often and lived just an hour away from them.

Amy reached the only conclusion she could think of: There was something seriously wrong with her. Not knowing what else to do, she made an appointment to see her pastor. Maybe he would refer her to a good psychologist.

"Loneliness is normal," he told her.

"No," she objected, "it's not normal for me. For loners, maybe, but I go out and have lots of friends. It's not as if I sit at home alone every night wishing someone would call. I go *out* every night." For the next half-hour, Amy listened and asked a lot of questions as her pastor explained how a person could be surrounded by people and still be lonely.

For most people loneliness is a condition that they would do everything in their power to overcome. Certainly, no one would actively seek out the empty feeling that loneliness creates. However, loneliness does serve a purpose in a believer's relationship with God, but each person must be willing to discover that purpose by spending time alone in His presence.

In everyone's life—believer and unbeliever alike—there's an empty place that only God can fill. Some people call it a "God-shaped hole," one that can only be filled when a person invites the Lord into his or her life. As time goes on, though, believers begin to sense an empty place opening up again. It's a place where God wants His children to experience a special intimacy with Him. If they aren't aware that God is beckoning them, they fill their lives up with activity and people and busyness.

Maybe your life is like Amy's—or maybe your postgraduation life has left you all alone in a strange town with no friends, no family, and few acquaintances. Most likely, though, your life is somewhere in between, with times of activity balanced by times of solitude. If so, you can be fairly certain that whatever loneliness you feel may be an indication that God wants more of you—more of your time, more of your focus, more of your love.

Then again, if you are lonely because you have cut yourself off from other people, your first order of business would be to ask God to give you the strength and direction to begin to open up to others. Loneliness is a common enough affliction; there's no need to arrange your life in such a way that you encourage it to dominate you. Reach out to others; just don't let your attempts at reaching out obscure the fact that you still need to spend time alone with God.

What should you during these special times with the Lord? You need to pray to invite Him to spend time with you, but after you do you might find that additional words are not necessary; simply *being* in His presence, silently allowing Him to minister to you, may make words irrelevant. You also might want to read a short passage of Scripture, reflecting on it and allowing God to reveal its truth to you. This is not the time for study or extensive reading; this is a time for relaxing and enjoying being with God the way you would enjoy being with a friend.

The people in your life can never fill up that place deep within you that is reserved for God alone; as Amy discovered as she sat in Starbucks with her friends. Keep your social life, but remember to invite Him to "socialize" with you alone.

I Will

Realize that loneliness is a normal part of living. *yes* _____ *no* _____

Avoid intentionally cutting myself off from other people. *yes* _____ *no* _____

Recognize the feeling of loneliness as a signal to spend time alone with God. *yes* _____ *no* _____

Give God more of my time, my attention, and my love. *yes* _____ *no* _____

Relax and simply *be* with God instead of thinking I have to *do* something all the time. *yes* _____ *no* _____

Understand that people can never fill the place in my life that belongs to God alone. *yes* _____ *no* _____

Things to Do

☐ *Think of the last time you experienced loneliness and decide if the method you used to overcome it worked.*

☐ *Write a poem or a short entry in your journal about how loneliness feels to you.*

☐ *Spend time alone with God, just being in His presence.*

☐ *If you are surrounded by friends, reach out to someone who seems lonely. If you are not, reach out to someone for the friendship you need.*

☐ *Make a list of the good things that loneliness compels you to do.*

☐ *Write a letter to God explaining how much you need to sense His presence when you are feeling lonely.*

Things to Remember

God said, "It is not good for the man to be alone. I will make a helper who is just right for him."

GENESIS 2:18 NIrV

[Jesus said,] "Therefore you now have sorrow; but I will see you again and your heart will rejoice, and your joy no one will take from you."

JOHN 16:22 NKJV

You will make me greater than ever, and you will comfort me again.
Psalm 71:21 NCV

[Jesus said to His disciples,] "Teach them to obey everything that I have taught you, and I will be with you always, even until the end of this age."

MATTHEW 28:20 NCV

God places the lonely in families; he sets the prisoners free and gives them joy. But for rebels, there is only famine and distress.

PSALM 68:6 NLT

[John said,] "God will wipe away every tear from their eyes; there shall be no more death, nor sorrow, nor crying. There shall be no more pain, for the former things have passed away."

REVELATION 21:4 NKJV

O may Your lovingkindness comfort me, according to Your word to Your servant.

PSALM 119:76 NASB

The ransomed of the LORD shall return, and come to Zion with singing, with everlasting joy on their heads. They shall obtain joy and gladness, and sorrow and sighing shall flee away.

ISAIAH 35:10 NKJV

Be merciful to me, O LORD, for I am in distress; my eyes grow weak with sorrow, my soul and my body with grief.

PSALM 31:9 NIV

Isn't God's comfort enough for you, even when gently spoken to you?

JOB 15:11 GOD'S WORD

Loneliness is only an opportunity to cut adrift and find yourself.

ANNE SHANNON MONROE

To most people loneliness is a doom. Yet loneliness is the very thing which God has chosen to be one of the schools of training for His very own. It is the fire that sheds the dross and reveals the gold.

BERNARD MARTIN

Second Chances

[Jesus said,] "Forgive people when they sin against you. If you do, your Father who is in heaven will also forgive you."

MATTHEW 6:14 NIrV

You just found out that your best friend betrayed a confidence. You trusted her; you believed in her; you shared your most private thoughts with her. How could she do this to you? You can't imagine ever speaking to her again. Yet . . . the Bible says you should forgive her.

More questions swirl around in your mind: *How can I possibly forgive her? How can God expect me to forgive her? Does He know what He's asking of me?*

Yes, God does know what He's asking of you. He knows how hard it can be at times for people to forgive each other. He also knows that you can forgive your friend, because He has given you the power to forgive. He knows that in forgiving others, you open yourself up to a steady stream of forgiveness flowing back your way. That's a lesson that will serve you well in the years to come.

Jesus was as clear about forgiveness as He was about any spiritual issue He addressed during His time on Earth. If you forgive those who have hurt you and betrayed you and sinned against you in any way, He said, God will forgive you. He considered this to be such a critical matter in the life of a believer that He made a point of emphasizing the link between forgiving others and receiving forgiveness from God in the model prayer He gave us, which we commonly call the Lord's Prayer: "Forgive us our sins, for we also forgive everyone who is indebted to us" (Luke 11:4 NKJV).

When you withhold forgiveness, you may think the only person you are hurting is the one who wronged you. But you are also hurting yourself by blocking the flow of forgiveness from God to you and by thwarting any hope of reconciliation with your friend. Until you forgive her, you will suffer the effects of a broken relationship just as much as she will.

Ask God to change your heart and show you how to access the power He has given you to forgive. Be open to the possibility that what seemed to be a betrayal may actually be a misunderstanding. Give God the opportunity to do the work of reconciliation between you and your friend—and between God and you. Forgive your friend—"seventy times seven" times, if necessary, as Jesus instructed in Matthew 18. In so doing you will demolish the blockage that prevented God's forgiveness from being activated in your life.

I Will

Have an attitude of forgiveness toward anyone who has wronged me.

_____ yes _____ no

Understand the connection between my forgiveness of others and God's forgiveness of me.

_____ yes _____ no

Strive for reconciliation when a relationship has been broken.

_____ yes _____ no

Allow God to change my heart.

_____ yes _____ no

Be thankful for God's forgiveness.

_____ yes _____ no

Realize that withholding forgiveness hurts me as well as others.

_____ yes _____ no

Things to Do

☐ *Pray the Lord's Prayer, found in Matthew 6:9–13.*

☐ *Make a list of people you feel you need to forgive. If appropriate, forgive them directly. If not, express your forgiveness to God.*

☐ *Thank God for the many times He has forgiven you for the sins you have committed.*

☐ *Find an image of Thomas Blackshear's painting* Forgiven *on the Web and write down what comes to mind as you look at it.*

☐ *Read about King David and how forgiveness figured so prominently in his life, in 2 Samuel 11–12.*

☐ *Write out your own definition of forgiveness.*

Things to Remember

[Jesus said,] "I assure you that any sin can be forgiven."

MARK 3:28 NLT

Be kind and tender to one another. Forgive each other, just as God forgave you because of what Christ has done.

EPHESIANS 4:32 NIrV

[Jesus said,] "Forgive us our sins, for we also forgive everyone who is indebted to us."

LUKE 11:4 NKJV

[The LORD said,] "The past troubles will be forgotten and hidden from my eyes."

ISAIAH 65:16 NIV

Then Peter came to Jesus and asked, "Lord, how many times shall I forgive my brother when he sins against me? Up to seven times?" Jesus answered, "I tell you, not seven times, but seventy-seven times."

MATTHEW 18:21–22 NIV

[Jesus said,] "When you are praying, first forgive anyone you are holding a grudge against, so that your Father in heaven will forgive your sins, too."

MARK 11:25 NLT

The glory of Christianity is to conquer by forgiveness.

WILLIAM BLAKE

Forgiveness does not change the past, but it does enlarge the future.

PAUL BOESE

Making Friends

The First Move

Godly people are careful about the friends they choose. But the way of sinners leads them down the wrong path.

PROVERBS 12:26 NIrV

After three months at her new school, Beth had to admit that she had not made a single friend. What was wrong? She thought she was pleasant enough—no major personality disorders, gross habits, or antisocial ways. Everyone was nice to her—that wasn't the problem—but she hadn't really clicked with any of the other girls. This wasn't the way she expected college to be.

No matter which way you're heading after graduation, you may be wondering if you will find yourself to be friendless at some point. You've heard conflicting myths: "Don't worry about it. You'll have more friends than you'll know what to do with," versus "You never know whom you can trust. It's next to impossible to make new friends."

The truth lies somewhere in between. Like everyone else, you'll never have more friends than you know what to do with, and you will find people you can trust. However, a new environment can be disorienting, so you may feel nervous and a bit detached from the others at first. A new environment can also be exciting, and if you approach your new life with that attitude, you'll find it easier to relax and feel more comfortable mingling with all those strangers around you.

For any friendship to happen, someone has to make the first move. It might as well be you—but don't think you have to make a big move. Start out small. Take the initiative and introduce yourself. Invite someone out for coffee or practice hospitality in your own apartment. Get involved in an activity that would be likely to attract people with interests similar to yours: a book club, a softball team, a photography class, or any other group activity that you enjoy.

As you begin to feel more comfortable with the people around you, try starting a Bible study group related to your field of interest—creation or literature, for instance. If you're not going to continue your education, you may want to start a neighborhood Bible study using a more generic topic, such as one of the Gospels. Practice hospitality in whatever way you are able; keep it simple and casual and comfortable for everyone.

Genuine friendships take time, and deep friendships take even more time. Don't be discouraged if, like Beth, you find it more difficult to make new friends than you thought it would be. In many areas of your life, you are having to start all over again, and that includes your social life. Give yourself time to adjust; friendships will come soon enough.

I Will

Remember that friendships take time to develop.   yes   no

Learn to practice Christian hospitality.   yes   no

Entrust my social life to God.   yes   no

View my new life as exciting.   yes   no

Take the initiative in reaching out to others.   yes   no

Realize that I need time to adjust to my new environment.   yes   no

Refuse to become discouraged.   yes   no

Things to Do

☐ *Invite a potential friend out for coffee this week.*

☐ *Ask God to help you as you try to make new friends.*

☐ *Participate in an activity that would attract people with interests similar to yours.*

☐ *Find written or online Bible study materials that you would feel comfortable using if you decide to start a group in the future.*

☐ *Make a list of ways that you can practice hospitality, even if money is tight and you live in a dorm.*

☐ *Think back to how you've made friends in the past and apply those principles to your present situation.*

Things to Remember

Some friendships do not last, but some friends are more loyal than brothers.

PROVERBS 18:24 GNT

I thank my God upon every remembrance of you.

PHILIPPIANS 1:3 NKJV

A friend loves at all times. He is there to help when trouble comes.

PROVERBS 17:17 NIrV

As iron sharpens iron, so one person sharpens another.

PROVERBS 27:17 NIrV

David finished talking to Saul. After that, Jonathan became David's closest friend. He loved David as much as [he loved] himself.

1 SAMUEL 18:1 GOD'S WORD

David said, "Is there still anyone who is left of the house of Saul, that I may show him kindness for Jonathan's sake?"

2 SAMUEL 9:1 NKJV

Friendship improves happiness, and abates misery, by doubling our joys, and dividing our grief.

JOSEPH ADDISON

The world is round so that friendship may encircle it.

PIERRE TEILHARD DE CHARDIN

Consequences

Who Cares?

A prudent person foresees the danger ahead and takes precautions; the simpleton goes blindly on and suffers the consequences.

—PROVERBS 22:3 NLT

Throughout high school, Kaitlyn had been a model student, with better-than-average grades and no demerits for breaking the rules. She was well-liked by her teachers and worked in her guidance counselor's office during lunchtime. Like the other seniors, she looked forward to graduation, which was just a week away.

Stopping at her locker before her English final, Kaitlyn opened her backpack. A bottle of ibuprofen fell out—and rolled across the floor, right in front of Officer Mac, the school resource officer. Mac had no choice; picking up the bottle of painkillers, he motioned to Kaitlyn, who followed him to the guidance office. There, the vice-principal repeated the school's zero-tolerance policy with regard to drugs. No drugs of any kind—including over-the-counter medicines—were allowed on campus unless they were to be administered by the school nurse.

Kaitlyn tried to explain: She had used her backpack over the weekend when she spent the night at a friend's house; she just forgot to remove the ibuprofen. But zero tolerance meant zero tolerance. Kaitlyn's parents were called, and she was forced to leave school immediately. She would not be allowed to attend graduation. She would receive her diploma after she completed her finals—over the summer.

Sound unfair? Everyone from the highest school official, to Kaitlyn's friends, family, and teachers, to the local newspaper agreed that her punishment was unfair. It was school policy, and this was one policy that had no give in it. It was more rigid than any other policy on the books. There was no procedure Kaitlyn could use to appeal her punishment.

Actions have consequences, sometimes far more severe than anyone can anticipate or imagine. The school board did not anticipate a situation in which a student like Kaitlyn would be the first to violate—and therefore test—the zero-tolerance drug policy. Kaitlyn could not imagine being forced to sit out her high school graduation over a moment of forgetfulness.

No doubt about it, life can serve up some bitter medicine at times. Suffering the consequences of your actions may not always include swallowing medicine as bitter as Kaitlyn's, but the punishment can still be unpleasant. Sometimes the only consequence may be losing your peace with God, but often, that's plenty.

You already know that God is a forgiving God, rich in mercy and grace. You know that when you have messed up in any way, you can confess your error to God, ask for His forgiveness, and immediately be forgiven. His mercy and grace will be extended to you. But you still may have to face the consequences of your actions.

Here's an example of what that means. On several occasions Mike had used his father's car without permission. To Mike, it was no big deal; he always drove responsibly and replaced the gas he used, and his father never seemed to suspect that Mike had driven the car. But on one perfectly clear day when his father had taken the train to work, Mike was driving his dad's car to a friend's house when another driver ran a stop sign, causing a minor wreck.

A remorseful Mike expected the worst, but after his father calmed down, he forgave his son and extended grace and mercy to him by not imposing any severe restrictions on him. But Mike still had to suffer the consequences by paying for the repair work. In addition, the insurance premiums on the car increased, and Mike had to pay for the difference between the old and new rates as well.

Had Mike heeded Proverbs 22:3, he could have avoided the consequences altogether, because he would have "[foreseen] the danger ahead and [taken] precautions"—by never driving his father's car without permission. As you venture out into the world on your own, you will become increasingly responsible for foreseeing the danger ahead and taking precautions to avoid wrong actions that will result in unpleasant or severe consequences—like losing your peace with God and having a guilty conscience.

Increase your awareness of what the Word of God has to say about the dangers that always accompany sin. Steer clear of the painful consequences of sin by steering clear of sin itself. Life may serve up some bitter medicine, as it did with Kaitlyn, but you can avoid lots of doses of that medicine by focusing on the prevention.

I Will

Understand that my actions have consequences. _yes_ _no_

Increase my awareness of what the Bible says about sin. _yes_ _no_

Learn to foresee the danger ahead. _yes_ _no_

Steer clear of painful consequences by steering clear of sin. _yes_ _no_

Realize that one of the results of sin is losing my peace with God. _yes_ _no_

Enjoy the pleasure of having a clear conscience. _yes_ _no_

Things to Do

☐ *Read about the consequences of sin in the story of David and Bathsheba in 2 Samuel 11–12.*

☐ *In your journal, write about a time when you had to suffer the consequences of your misguided actions.*

☐ *Memorize Proverbs 22:3.*

☐ *Thank God for sending the Holy Spirit to warn you in advance of the dangers ahead.*

☐ *Select one of the quotations on the following page and write about what it means to you.*

☐ *Make sure you understand how you can receive God's mercy and grace and still be responsible for paying the consequences of sin.*

Things to Remember

To Adam [the LORD said], "Because you listened to your wife and ate the fruit I told you not to eat, I have placed a curse on the ground. All your life you will struggle to scratch a living from it."

GENESIS 3:17 NLT

Peter said to [Simon the Sorcerer], "Your money perish with you, because you thought that the gift of God could be purchased with money! You have neither part nor portion in this matter, for your heart is not right in the sight of God."

ACTS 8:20–21 NKJV

The wages of sin is death, but the gift of God is eternal life in Christ Jesus our Lord.

Romans 6:23 NKJV

[John wrote,] Dear friends, if our hearts do not condemn us, we have confidence before God and receive from him anything we ask, because we obey his commands and do what pleases him.

1 JOHN 3:21–22 NIV

"I, the LORD, search the minds and hearts of people. I treat each of them according to the way they live."

JEREMIAH 17:10 GNT

[Jesus said,] "Suppose someone welcomes a prophet as a prophet. That one will receive a prophet's reward. And suppose someone welcomes a godly person as a godly person. That one will receive a godly person's reward. Suppose someone gives even a cup of cold water to a little one who follows me. What I'm about to tell you is true. That one will certainly be rewarded."

MATTHEW 10:41–42 NIrV

Be sure to give to them without any hesitation. When you do this the LORD your God will bless you in everything you work for and set out to do.

DEUTERONOMY 15:10 GOD'S WORD

[Daniel said,] "My God sent his angel to close the lions' mouths. They have not hurt me, because my God knows I am innocent. I never did anything wrong to you, O king." King Darius was very happy and told his servants to lift Daniel out of the lions' den. So they lifted him out and did not find any injury on him, because Daniel had trusted in his God.

DANIEL 6:22–23 NCV

It is easy to dodge our responsibilities, but we cannot dodge the consequences of dodging our responsibilities.

SIR JOSIAH STAMP

Sometimes when I consider what tremendous consequences come from little things, I am tempted to think there are no little things.

BRUCE BARTON

Goals

Your Personal Adviser

Brethren, I do not count myself to have apprehended; but one thing I do, forgetting those things which are behind and reaching forward to those things which are ahead, I press toward the goal for the prize of the upward call of God in Christ Jesus.

PHILIPPIANS 3:13–14 NKJV

Anyone who has made it as far as graduation has had some practice in setting goals, and you are no exception. If your school gave specific instruction and encouragement on goal-setting, you are ahead of the game.

Setting goals can be a setup for discouragement, though, if you have no way of measuring your progress. If your main goal in life is to be a better Christian, that's certainly admirable. But it's not a goal you complete and then go on to something else. It's a lifelong, progressive activity, which means that you need to engage in regular spiritual practices that will contribute toward deepening your relationship with Christ.

Some goals are more clearly measurable, but even

with those you need to be careful not to set yourself up for frustration. Is your goal to be the top software designer for a major game company? What will it take to reach that goal? Break that larger goal down into smaller steps. Each step will become a goal in itself. The feeling of satisfaction and fulfillment you will get as you reach each smaller goal will propel you to the next step.

In some cases a goal can best be achieved by creating deadlines for meeting different milestones along the way. Maybe you want to work at a major metropolitan newspaper. Your timeline may look like this: four years of college, one year as a reporter on a small-town newspaper, earn a master's degree, three years on a medium-sized paper, land a job at the *Los Angeles Times.* You may accomplish all that in less time, but in setting a realistic schedule, you are doing yourself a favor by warding off discouragement.

Whether you are setting short-term or long-range goals, whether your goals relate to your spiritual life or your career or your relationships, the best adviser you can consult during the process is God. He is the one who knows you best, who knows what is best for you, who knows how you can make the best use of your talents and your time on Earth. Maintain a prayerful attitude whenever you consider your future and what you want for it; God will guide you every step of the way.

Make sure you celebrate each time you meet a goal, no matter how small that goal may be. It's important to recognize those milestones, because they keep you fueled and energized over the long haul. Be sure to bring God into the celebration by thanking Him for His help.

I Will

Rely on God to help me set and meet my goals.   _yes_   _no_

Ward off discouragement by breaking large goals into smaller ones.   _yes_   _no_

Realize that some spiritual goals will take longer to reach than others will.   _yes_   _no_

Acknowledge the importance of measuring my progress in meeting my goals.   _yes_   _no_

Make sure the goals I set are realistic and attainable.   _yes_   _no_

Maintain a prayerful attitude whenever I consider my future.   _yes_   _no_

Be grateful to God for helping me achieve my goals.   _yes_   _no_

Things to Do

☐ *Identify a goal you have already met and identify the individual steps it took to achieve it.*

☐ *Create a timetable for meeting your career goals. Keep it flexible and realistic.*

☐ *Set several spiritual goals, listing the activities (such as prayer and Bible study) you will need to engage in as you progress toward those goals.*

☐ *Make a list of your most significant relationships; next to each name write a corresponding goal (such as reconciliation, deeper trust level, forgiveness).*

☐ *Brainstorm with a friend about your more abstract goals—such as making your life more meaningful—and concrete ways you can meet them.*

Things to Remember

The Lord says, "I will make you wise and show you where to go. I will guide you and watch over you."

PSALM 32:8 NCV

This God is our God for ever and ever. He will be our guide to the very end.

PSALM 48:14 NIrV

Ask the LORD to bless your plans, and you will be successful in carrying them out.

PROVERBS 16:3 GNT

All who are led by the Spirit of God are children of God.

ROMANS 8:14 NLT

Do not be foolish but learn what the Lord wants you to do.

EPHESIANS 5:17 NCV

[Paul wrote,] So I run—but not without a clear goal ahead of me. So I box—but not as if I were just shadow boxing.

1 CORINTHIANS 9:26 GOD'S WORD

If you're bored with life—you don't get up every morning with a burning desire to do things—you don't have enough goals.

LOU HOLTZ

Goals are dreams with deadlines.

DIANA SCHARF HUNT

Gratitude

Fall on Your Knees

Let the word of Christ dwell in you richly; teach and admonish one another in all wisdom; and with gratitude in your hearts sing psalms, hymns, and spiritual songs to God.

COLOSSIANS 3:16 NRSV

If you had a dollar for every time your mother told you to say "Thank you," you would probably have enough money to live on for months. And thank-you notes. Every Christmas and birthday, there was your mother, pen and paper in hand, telling you to sit down and write that note before you do another thing.

You're on your own now, and you don't have anyone hovering over you, making sure you say the right things and use your very best penmanship. You'll have to figure out a way to remember to thank all the people you should and send all those thank-you notes before the next big holiday or milestone in your life rolls around.

It's not hard to remember to thank people if you've cultivated a grateful attitude. Thankfulness springs from a heart that recognizes the good things that have come your way, things that you possibly never asked for and never thought you deserved.

Remembering to thank people may come naturally to you, but it can't hurt to stop and assess how you're doing when it comes to expressing your gratitude. Are you specific in mentioning *what* you're thankful for? "Thanks for the dc Talk CD" shows you paid attention to what the giver gave; "Thanks for the gift" does not. Do you thank people in a timely manner? It helps to have note cards and stamps on hand. In this day of hastily written e-mails, a handwritten card is a rare treat.

Of course, the largest portion of your gratitude should go to God. Never pass up an opportunity to thank Him; there's no way you can overdo it. He deserves more of your gratitude than you can ever express.

Assess how you're doing when it comes to thanking Him too. Are you specific with God? It's OK to thank Him for everything He's done for you, but "Thank You for giving me a clear mind during finals" acknowledges His activity in your daily life. Do you thank Him in a timely manner? Thank Him as soon as you recognize His hand in some area of your life. That way, you won't forget it later on, and you will continually be aware of the ways He intervenes in your life.

A grateful attitude is a sign of both humility and maturity. As you learn to live life on your own, acknowledging the many things God and other people have done for you will help keep you humble as you grow spiritually and emotionally.

I Will

Be grateful to God at all times.
_____ *yes* _____ *no*

Be thankful toward other people.
_____ *yes* _____ *no*

Recognize the good and undeserved things that have come my way.
_____ *yes* _____ *no*

Realize that thankfulness is a sign of humility and maturity.
_____ *yes* _____ *no*

Acknowledge God's activity in my daily life.
_____ *yes* _____ *no*

Remember to express my gratitude in a timely way.
_____ *yes* _____ *no*

Assess how I am doing when it comes to thanking God and others.
_____ *yes* _____ *no*

Things to Do

☐ *Buy a set of note cards and a book of stamps to keep on hand for sending thank-you notes.*

☐ *Write thank-you notes this week to two people who have done something good for you that you never thanked them for.*

☐ *In your journal, start a list of specific things for which you are grateful to God.*

☐ *Pray Psalm 95:1–7 back to God.*

☐ *Write "Have I failed to thank anyone today?" on an index card and tape it where you will see it each night before you go to sleep.*

☐ *Read about Jesus' encounter with the thankful Samaritan in Luke 17:12–19.*

Things to Remember

Then you will sing psalms and hymns and spiritual songs among yourselves, making music to the Lord in your hearts. And you will always give thanks for everything to God the Father in the name of our Lord Jesus Christ.

EPHESIANS 5:19–20 NLT

Oh come, let us sing to the LORD! Let us shout joyfully to the Rock of our salvation. Let us come before His presence with thanksgiving; let us shout joyfully to Him with psalms.

PSALM 95:1–2 NKJV

O give thanks to the LORD, for He is good; for His lovingkindness is everlasting.

1 CHRONICLES 16:34 NASB

Since we are receiving a kingdom that cannot be shaken, let us be thankful, and so worship God acceptably with reverence and awe.

HEBREWS 12:28 NIV

If God gives us wealth and property and lets us enjoy them, we should be grateful and enjoy what we have worked for. It is a gift from God.

ECCLESIASTES 5:19 GNT

Thankfulness may consist merely of words. Gratitude is shown in acts.

HENRI FREDERIC AMIEL

Gratitude is a twofold love—love coming to visit us, and love running out to greet a welcome guest.

HENRY VAN DYKE

Laying the Foundation

Brick by Brick

Let [the wealthy] do good, that they be rich in good works, ready to give, willing to share, storing up for themselves a good foundation for the time to come, that they may lay hold on eternal life.

1 TIMOTHY 6:18–19 NKJV

Do you know someone who is a builder? If so, you can be sure that they will tell you that the single most important part of any building is the foundation. No matter how strong the framework is, the building will not withstand pressure and stress if the foundation is not properly designed to support it. Start with a solid foundation, and you stand a much better chance of building a structure that will last.

Your life must also have a solid foundation if you are to survive the stresses that will come your way. How can you be sure that the foundation of your life is strong enough? There's one basis for life that has withstood the tests of time and of truth, and that is the gospel of Jesus Christ. When you build on that basis, there's a greater likelihood that you will withstand the pressures you will inevitably face in the coming years.

Maybe you already have a strong foundation. You have believed in Jesus for years and have learned to trust Him in increasingly deeper ways. Still, it may be time for a little building inspection. Do you have an unshakeable understanding of who God is and how He works in your life? Do you believe that the Bible is the Word of God and can be trusted to provide guidance and wisdom throughout your life? Do you regularly attend a church that preaches the gospel of Christ? Are the main influences in your life people who believe as you do? Your answers to these questions and others will provide clues to just how solid the foundation of your life is.

Those questions also apply if you have come to a life of faith more recently. To lay a strong foundation for the rest of your life, you need to be sure that you have a clear understanding about, and belief in, God and the Bible as well as a commitment to aligning yourself with a Bible-believing church and like-minded friends. All of those factors contribute to shaping your adult life and provide a solid base on which you can build the life and mission God has for you.

Now that you are graduating and entering a new phase of your life, you need to be especially sure that the foundation you are building on is your own and not your parents'. As the saying goes, God has no grandchildren—only children. If your faith as a Christian is merely an inherited faith—in other words, if you haven't examined the claims of Christ for yourself, if you believe in Him only because your parents did—then your foundation will not be strong enough to bear the weight of what you will face in the future. You need to personally place each brick, each stone, each cement block of your own foundation.

If you're not sure where to start in laying a foundation—or in inspecting the one you've already placed—ask your pastor or youth leader to recommend a good foundational Bible study. Many free studies are available online or through the mail from ministries, missions, and other Christian organizations. Excellent basic Bible studies can also be found at your local Christian bookstore. Be on the lookout, too, for group Bible study courses such as Alpha that are available at local churches.

Remember that nothing can equal the value of regularly spending personal time with God and with His Word. You may not always have a structured course available to you, but you will always have access to the presence of God and to His Word, to the extent to which you have learned it, memorized it, and incorporated it into the fabric of your everyday life. Your willingness and ability to go to God and draw on His wisdom and direction will give you strength throughout your life.

The Greek philosopher Socrates once said, "The unexamined life is not worth living." For the Christian the unexamined faith is not worth much. Examine your faith. Inspect your foundation. Be absolutely certain that all the basic building blocks of faith in Christ are in place in your life. When you can say that they are, you can look forward to your postgraduation future with confidence, knowing that the life you build will be able to withstand the most powerful assaults against it.

I Will

Be aware of the importance of a solid basis of faith for my life.

yes _____ _no_ _____

Lay a strong foundation for my life.

yes _____ _no_ _____

Make sure that my faith is my own and not an unexamined replica of my parents' faith.

yes _____ _no_ _____

Place a high priority on spending personal time with God and in His Word.

yes _____ _no_ _____

Regularly inspect the foundation of my life to see if there are any cracks in my faith that need to be sealed up.

yes _____ _no_ _____

Things to Do

☐ _Answer the questions posed in paragraph three._

☐ _Obtain a basic Bible study or enroll in a foundational course._

☐ _Ask God to show you any missing elements in your foundation of faith._

☐ _Make a written commitment to spend time with God every day. Sign it and date it._

☐ _Read what Jesus had to say about a strong foundation in Luke 6._

☐ _Memorize Ephesians 2:19–22._

☐ _Practice expressing your basic beliefs as a Christian until you feel you can adequately communicate them to someone else._

Things to Remember

This now is what the Sovereign LORD says: "I am placing in Zion a foundation that is firm and strong. In it I am putting a solid cornerstone on which are written the words, 'Faith that is firm is also patient.' "

ISAIAH 28:16 GNT

When the whirlwind passes, the wicked is no more, but the righteous has an everlasting foundation.

PROVERBS 10:25 NASB

> *Unless the Lord builds the house, they labor in vain who build it; unless the Lord guards the city, the watchman keeps awake in vain.*
>
> Psalm 127:1 NASB

Leaving the elementary teaching about the Christ, let us press on to maturity, not laying again a foundation of repentance from dead works and of faith toward God, of instruction about washings and laying on of hands, and the resurrection of the dead, and eternal judgment.

HEBREWS 6:1–2 NASB

[Jesus said,] "Some people come to me and listen to me and do what I say. I will show you what they are like. They are like someone who builds a house. He digs down deep and sets it on solid rock. When a flood comes, the river rushes against the house. But the water can't shake it. The house is well built."

LUKE 6:47–48 NIrV

[Paul wrote,] We are partners working together for God, and you are God's field. You are also God's building. Using the gift that God gave me, I did the work of an expert builder and laid the foundation, and someone else is building on it. But each of you must be careful how you build.

1 CORINTHIANS 3:9–10 GNT

[The LORD said,] "[My people] will build houses and inhabit them; they will also plant vineyards and eat their fruit. They will not build and another inhabit, they will not plant and another eat; for as the lifetime of a tree, so will be the days of My people, and My chosen ones will wear out the work of their hands."

ISAIAH 65:21–22 NASB

[Jesus said,] "If one of you is planning to build a tower, you sit down first and figure out what it will cost, to see if you have enough money to finish the job. If you don't, you will not be able to finish the tower after laying the foundation; and all who see what happened will make fun of you. 'You began to build but can't finish the job!' they will say."

LUKE 14:28–30 GNT

Character is the foundation stone upon which one must build to win respect. Just as no worthy building can be erected on a weak foundation, so no lasting reputation worthy of respect can be built on a weak character.

R. C. SAMSEL

If you don't have solid beliefs you cannot build a stable life. Beliefs are like the foundation of a building, and they are the foundation to build your life upon.

ALFRED A. MONTAPERT

Honesty

High Standards

No one who lies and cheats will live in my house. No one who tells lies will serve me.

PSALM 101:7 NIrV

You're an honest person, right? You don't cheat on tests or take money from the cash register at work or shoplift from Wal-Mart. You would never think to do those things. You're a decent person. You follow the rules. You obey the laws.

Even so, subtle ways of being dishonest can sneak up on people of integrity. Now that you no longer have teachers and school resource officers and your parents watching your every move, you are more vulnerable to the subtle temptation to fudge a little on the truth now and then. Some people rationalize away those "minor indiscretions," but make no mistake about it: Lying and dishonesty are serious issues to God.

You know when you are about to cross a line that you should never cross. You're on the phone with a friend who can't stop talking about his car; to end the conversation, you start to tell him you have to get to class. He doesn't know that you don't have any more classes that day. Go ahead and get off the phone, but don't grieve the God you love and serve by telling a lie. Between your creative thinking skills and all the words in the English language, you can manage to hang up without lying to your friend, angering him, or insulting him.

Ask God to show you how you are most vulnerable to dishonesty, and be on guard whenever such a situation arises. Pray that the Holy Spirit would tweak your conscience before you say anything that is not true—or anything that would be unnecessarily hurtful to another person. Sometimes confronting people with the truth about the sin in their lives causes temporary pain. But speaking the whole truth and nothing but the truth doesn't mean that you need to tell Aunt Edna that her shoes make her look dumpy.

Adhering to a high standard of honesty is not always easy. You will face many situations in which telling a white lie is easier than telling the truth. But dishonesty is one of the sins that can quickly become a habit—so quickly that you may not be fully aware of the damage it has done, or you have done, until it is too late. The God who has always been honest and forthright with you wants you to be honest and forthright with Him and with others. So much so, in fact, that He gives you the power to maintain a standard of truthfulness in all you do and say.

I Will

Adhere to a high standard of honesty. _____ yes _____ no

Recognize the immediate habit-forming nature of
dishonesty. _____ yes _____ no

Be careful not to use the truth to hurt people. _____ yes _____ no

Draw on God's power to be truthful in all I say
and do. _____ yes _____ no

Be aware of those situations in which I am
vulnerable to being dishonest. _____ yes _____ no

Realize that God takes lying and dishonesty seriously. _____ yes _____ no

Be thankful that God has always been honest and
forthright with me. _____ yes _____ no

Things to Do

☐ *Think of the last time you did something dishonest and make it right
through confession and restitution, if necessary.*

☐ *Discuss honesty with a close friend and resolve to hold each other
accountable when it comes to telling the truth.*

☐ *Use a concordance to find verses about dishonesty, concentrating on
the book of Proverbs, for a quick study on the biblical view of lying.*

☐ *Memorize Colossians 3:9–10, meditating on how it applies to your
"new life"—in Christ and as a recent graduate.*

☐ *Write in your journal about how you could be more honest.*

☐ *Read the story of Ananias and Sapphira in Acts 5:1–11 to see how
seriously God dealt with their sin of lying.*

Things to Remember

Lying lips are an abomination to the LORD, but those who deal faithfully are His delight.

PROVERBS 12:22 NASB

Pray for us, for we are sure that we have a good conscience, desiring to conduct ourselves honorably in all things.

HEBREWS 13:18 NASB

Do not cheat one another. Do not lie.

LEVITICUS 19:11 NLT

Who has the right to go up the LORD's hill? Who may enter his holy Temple? Those who are pure in act and in thought, who do not worship idols or make false promises.

PSALM 24:3–4 GNT

Don't lie to one another. You have gotten rid of your old way of life and its habits. You have started living a new life. It is being made new so that what you know has the Creator's likeness.

COLOSSIANS 3:9–10 NIrV

Wealth you get by dishonesty will do you no good, but honesty can save your life.

PROVERBS 10:2 GNT

Honesty is the first chapter of the book of wisdom.

THOMAS JEFFERSON

The true measure of life is not length, but honesty.

JOHN LYLY

Hope

Never Give Up

Therefore, prepare your minds for action; be self-controlled; set your hope fully on the grace to be given you when Jesus Christ is revealed.

1 PETER 1:13 NIV

"I hope I get a high-paying job after I graduate."

"I hope I get accepted at the USC grad school."

"I hope my unit gets called up to fight terrorism."

That's how people typically use the word *hope* these days—to describe the way they wish for something to happen. That "something" can either be likely to happen, such as getting a certain job for which you are highly qualified, or unlikely to happen, such as winning a $32 million lottery that you never play.

But hope in the biblical sense means something a whole lot better than mere wishing. The word *hope* describes the certainty you can have that the promises of God will come to pass. While those outside the community of faith must pin their hopes on such dubious factors as the goodness of humankind or the benevolence of governments or the faithfulness of politicians, those who believe in Christ can fasten their hope on the one sure thing in life, the goodness and benevolence and faithfulness of God.

Your hope in God should be at an all-time high right about now. He has faithfully brought you to this milestone in your life, one that positions you for perhaps the biggest change you have ever known. Graduation speakers tend to underscore the magnitude of this step in your life; phrases like "endless possibilities" and "limitless potential" pepper their speeches, buoying your already uplifted spirits. If you envision your future against a backdrop of faith, your hope in God can't help but soar.

Keep that hope in God always before you. It can help you get through your everyday life, as you cling to the hope that God's promises for your earthly existence will come to pass. Daily reminders of your hope in God can counteract the effects of the negatives life sends your way, like failure and disappointments and emotional turmoil and physical pain. Likewise, the hope of heaven and eternal life provides you with a peace of mind that helps temper the anxiety that the fear of death can produce.

Don't be surprised if you experience times when your hope starts to sag. That happens to the most faithful of believers. Hold on to the truth that God's promises will be fulfilled. Ask Him to restore the hope that seems to have disappeared. No matter what, never give up. Your hope in God represents certainty, not wishful thinking.

I Will

Keep my hope in God always before me.   _____ yes   _____ no

Believe that God's promises for my earthly life will
be fulfilled.   _____ yes   _____ no

Look forward to the hope of heaven.   _____ yes   _____ no

Fasten my hope on the one sure thing in life, God.   _____ yes   _____ no

Envision my future against a backdrop of faith
in God.   _____ yes   _____ no

Turn to God immediately if my hope starts to sag.   _____ yes   _____ no

Never give up.   _____ yes   _____ no

Things to Do

☐ Pray Psalm 33, a psalm of hope, back to God.

☐ In your journal, start a list of your hopes—the deep longings of your
spirit that only God can satisfy.

☐ Meditate on the hope of eternal life that God has given you.

☐ Create a hope chest out of a shoebox: write down Bible verses about
hope, place them in the box, and read them when you get discouraged.

☐ Thank God for the certain hope you have in Him.

☐ Share the hope you have in Christ with one other person.

☐ Read Paul's letter to the Romans, noting his frequent references
to hope.

Things to Remember

We were saved in this hope, but hope that is seen is not hope; for why does one still hope for what he sees?

ROMANS 8:24 NKJV

Wait . . . for God. Wait with hope. Hope now; hope always!

PSALM 131:3 THE MESSAGE

I'm a hostage here for hope, not doom.

ACTS 28:20 THE MESSAGE

When the true message, the Good News, first came to you, you heard about the hope it offers. So your faith and love are based on what you hope for, which is kept safe for you in heaven.

COLOSSIANS 1:5 GNT

If we hope for what we do not yet have, we wait for it patiently.

ROMANS 8:25 NIV

These two things cannot change: God cannot lie when he makes a promise, and he cannot lie when he makes an oath. These things encourage us who came to God for safety. They give us strength to hold on to the hope we have been given. We have this hope as an anchor for the soul, sure and strong.

HEBREWS 6:18–19 NCV

> Faith means believing the unbelievable. Hope means hoping when everything seems hopeless.
>
> GILBERT K. CHESTERTON

> If it were not for hopes, the heart would break.
>
> THOMAS FULLER

Accountability

Nitty-Gritty Confession

Let each of you look out not only for his own interests, but also for the interests of others.

PHILIPPIANS 2:4 NKJV

Rachel had gone off to college with the kind of enthusiasm you would expect from a freshman on her own for the first time. She had looked forward to the fact that there would be no one to get on her case to wake up in time for class or even to attend her classes, for that matter. She could stay out as late as she wanted and come and go as she pleased. But she had wanted to prove to herself that she was a responsible adult, so at first she did a pretty good job of adjusting to her new life of freedom.

Determined to keep her spiritual life from taking a hit, Rachel began attending the meetings of one of the more active Christian fellowships on campus. There, she made a few friends, but none of them were in her classes or lived in her dorm. At first she would get together every now and then with her friends at a local café, but eventually Rachel's schedule got in the way. When she stopped attending the larger fellowship meetings altogether, a few of the students called to make sure she was doing all right. She was just busy, she said, assuring them that she was

OK. She believed it herself; after all, she still went to church most Sundays. What she didn't notice was that she had drifted away from the very people who had kept her grounded in her faith during this crucial time in her life. As a consequence, her spiritual life had taken the hit she had wanted to avoid.

The small group of friends that met for coffee was probably more vital to Rachel's spiritual life than she realized. With the right focus, and an understanding of the need to be accountable to another believer, that small circle could have become a much-needed accountability group for Rachel and her friends. Several were sophomores who had survived freshman year with their faith intact; another was a freshman who, like Rachel, found herself making weekly, if not daily, adjustments to being on her own. All were part of a larger fellowship to whom they could turn for further help and encouragement.

Whether or not you are a part of an accountability group, you would do well to ask God to lead you to one person who would agree to be your accountability partner—an individual who is committed to living in right relationship to God and who will make a commitment to strengthen and encourage you in your own faith life, helping you to also stay in right relationship to God. Make sure you ask God to keep you committed to doing the same for your partner. Agree to meet regularly, and stick to that commitment as well.

Maybe like Rachel you thought you'd do fine on your own now that you're a bona fide adult. After a lifetime of having to answer to your parents, your teachers, and who knows how many other people, you may feel you shouldn't have to answer to anyone else for your personal life. If that's the way you see it, then you need to understand that accountability is not a punishment but a blessing. By making yourself accountable to one or more believers, you have a greater chance of maintaining your faith and high standards even as you experience the freedom you've wanted for so long. You get to return the favor when a brother or sister decides to be accountable to you.

For accountability to work you need to be open, honest, and vulnerable to your partner. That means getting down to the nitty-gritty sin and temptation in your life like you possibly never have before, and that requires an absolute commitment to confidentiality. Sometimes, confessing your sinful desires and actions out loud to another Christian—someone you trust completely—is enough to make you realize how close you may have come to falling away. As you pray together about the issues in your lives, you are releasing them to God in the presence of someone on Earth who is responsible for checking up on you. Knowing that even one other person is aware of your struggles, cares about them, and is praying for you can give you the strength to resist the temptations you face each day.

I Will

Make myself accountable to at least one other believer.

<u>*yes*</u> <u>*no*</u>

Encourage my friends to find an accountability partner.

<u>*yes*</u> <u>*no*</u>

Be honest and open about my struggles adjusting to my new independent lifestyle.

<u>*yes*</u> <u>*no*</u>

Remember that I also must answer to God.

<u>*yes*</u> <u>*no*</u>

Make myself available for someone else to be accountable to me.

<u>*yes*</u> <u>*no*</u>

Things to Do

☐ *Set up a regular schedule, like once a week, to meet with your accountability partner.*

☐ *Make a list of the most serious issues you encounter on a regular basis.*

☐ *Read Luke 17:1-10, where Jesus emphasized the responsibility to rebuke a sinning brother and forgive a repentant brother.*

☐ *Ask God to give you the grace and ability to maintain your commitment to confidentiality.*

☐ *List specific things you can do to avoid leaving yourself open to sinful desires and opportunities.*

☐ *Memorize Hebrews 4:13.*

☐ *Thank God for leading you on this pathway to spiritual growth.*

Things to Remember

Confess your sins to one another, and pray for one another, so that you may be healed. The prayer of the righteous is powerful and effective.

JAMES 5:16 NRSV

If someone in your group does something wrong, you who are spiritual should go to that person and gently help make him right again.

GALATIANS 6:1 NCV

Each of us will give an account of himself to God.
Romans 14:12 NIV

[Paul wrote,] We know that whatever the law says, it says to those who are under the law, so that every mouth may be silenced and the whole world held accountable to God.

ROMANS 3:19 NIV

[Job asked,] "What will I do when God confronts me? What will I answer when called to account?"

JOB 31:14 NIV

Why do the wicked renounce God, and say in their hearts, "You will not call us to account"?

PSALM 10:13 NRSV

[Jesus said,] "I tell you this, that you must give an account on judgment day of every idle word you speak."

MATTHEW 12:36 NLT

Obey those who rule over you, and be submissive, for they watch out for your souls, as those who must give account. Let them do so with joy and not with grief, for that would be unprofitable for you.

HEBREWS 13:17 NKJV

[Unbelievers] will give an account to Him who is ready to judge the living and the dead.

1 PETER 4:5 NKJV

The one who sins is the one who dies. The child will not be punished for the parent's sins, and the parent will not be punished for the child's sins. Righteous people will be rewarded for their own goodness, and wicked people will be punished for their own wickedness.

EZEKIEL 18:20 NLT

Good men prefer to be accountable.

MICHAEL EDWARDES

Life is not accountable to us. We are accountable to life.

DENIS WAITLEY

Humor

Laugh Track

[The LORD] will yet fill your mouth with laughing, and your lips with rejoicing.

JOB 8:21 NKJV

Someone thinks you need to be reminded to keep your sense of humor? That has to be a joke. You're the first one to laugh at a funny line in a movie or your friends' comical pranks. No way is your sense of humor going anywhere.

Hold on, though. You've probably already been confronted with academic policies that seem to make no sense and people who make unreasonable demands and a driver who cuts you off in an already tense traffic jam. Once you have graduated and are out on your own, you will come across annoying situations and people to an even greater degree. There's just no end to the potential for maddening encounters each day.

How will you respond when you've waited for an hour at the motor vehicle agency only to discover that the form you were told to fill out an hour earlier is not the right one—and you have to start the process all over again? Or when your landlord refuses to return your security deposit, claiming you are responsible for damage to the apartment that you left in perfect condition? Or when a police officer in another state pulls you over for an obscure traffic offense that your state wouldn't consider a violation?

Encounters like those can make your blood boil, but they are the stuff of everyday life as an adult. The way you respond to similar encounters can go a long way toward determining your quality of life, the impression you make on others, and even your own mental health. Keeping your "wit" about you— your sense of humor, that is—helps you to take maddening situations in stride, leave a favorable impression on others, and render powerless the kind of anger that can lead to cynicism, despair, and ultimately, depression.

Handling frustration with humor is not the same thing as shrugging off wrongs that should be made right. If you're being cheated by a dishonest landlord, for instance, you have every right to try to get your money back. Just make sure you do so with your peace of mind and your witness as a Christian intact. A good nature can accomplish much more than belligerence can, because it affects far more than just the end result.

Remember too that an appropriate sense of humor is never belittling or malicious or in any way demeaning to others. You can find the humor in any situation without being disrespectful. When you let God be the one to "fill your mouth with laughing," you can be certain that you're on the right laugh track.

I Will

Learn to laugh at maddening situations.   yes _____ no _____

Keep my good nature intact when I try to correct
a wrong.   yes _____ no _____

Maintain my witness as a Christian during difficult
encounters with others.   yes _____ no _____

Always use my sense of humor in appropriate ways.   yes _____ no _____

Trust God to teach me how to handle confrontation
in a respectful way.   yes _____ no _____

See the humor in situations that test my patience.   yes _____ no _____

Things to Do

☐ *Read the quotation by Percy Ross and think of a recent situation that would have turned out better if you had employed humor.*

☐ *Use a Christian search engine such as www.crosssearch.com to find Web sites devoted to "holy humor."*

☐ *Go through your day tomorrow determined to find the humor in annoying situations.*

☐ *Read about the positive effect of laughter on physical and emotional healing; sites like www.humorproject.com and www.humorforyourhealth.com are a good place to start.*

☐ *Thank God for giving you a healthy sense of humor.*

☐ *Use appropriate humor to help a friend who is going through a rough time.*

Things to Remember

[The psalmist wrote of the Israelites,] Our mouth was filled with laughter, and our tongue with singing. Then they said among the nations, "The LORD has done great things for them."

PSALM 126:2 NKJV

[Jesus said,] "Blessed are you who hunger now, for you shall be filled. Blessed are you who weep now, for you shall laugh."

LUKE 6:21 NKJV

A happy heart makes a face look cheerful, but a sad heart produces a broken spirit.

PROVERBS 15:13 NIrV

Sarah said, "God has made me laugh, and all who hear will laugh with me."

GENESIS 21:6 NKJV

[The LORD said,] "The people who live [in Jerusalem] will sing praise; they will shout for joy. By my blessing they will increase in numbers; my blessing will bring them honor."

JEREMIAH 30:19 GNT

A clever, imaginative, humorous request can open closed doors and closed minds.

PERCY ROSS

Delicate humor is the crowning virtue of the saints.

EVELYN UNDERHILL

Intellectual Life

Lifelong Learning

Teach the wise, and they will become even wiser; teach good people, and they will learn even more.

PROVERBS 9:9 NCV

Finally—graduation day has arrived. You can put away the textbooks, forget about cramming for tests, return all your extra reading material to the library, and never write another paper for as long as you live, right? That may be true if you are not going to continue with school. But while the schoolwork may come to an end, if you're smart, the learning never will.

Throughout your life, of course, you will continue to learn simply by having new experiences, going different places, and trying unfamiliar things. But to keep your mind sharp, learning must also be active and intentional. Researching a topic to satisfy your curiosity, determining your position on political or philosophical issues, and unraveling a knotty problem with a friend or coworker are all activities that involve full and active use of your intellect—along with a healthy dose of wisdom from God.

One of the most productive ways you can make use of the intelligence God gave you is by embarking on a lifelong study of His Word. Studying the Bible is far different from the devotional reading you do on a daily basis. Bible study can involve acquiring knowledge about a wide spectrum of subjects other than the Bible itself, such as everyday life in biblical times, the beliefs of surrounding cultures, the meanings of words in the original languages, archeological discoveries, and historical records from the biblical era.

In addition, commentaries and other reference materials written by biblical scholars are often helpful in studying the Word of God. All that may sound daunting, but don't worry—many people take a lifetime to accumulate such an extensive library of Bible study tools. The point is to start with what you already own and what you have available to you, such as online and library reference works. Never let an obstacle like not having the "right" book keep you from studying the Bible.

God created intelligence, and He gave you an intelligent mind to use, not to ignore. Show Him your appreciation by making the most of your brainpower in ways that honor Him and deepen your understanding of the universe He created. While you're at it, never lose sight of the simplicity of the gospel. Lifelong learning may lead you into complex areas of study, but the good news of Jesus Christ is not one of them.

I Will

Honor God by using the intelligence He has given me.

_____ yes   _____ no

See learning as a lifelong process, not a school-related activity.

_____ yes   _____ no

Realize the importance of intensive Bible study.

_____ yes   _____ no

Understand that some learning must be active and intentional if I want to keep my mind sharp.

_____ yes   _____ no

See the need for both devotional Bible reading and Bible study.

_____ yes   _____ no

Resist the temptation to complicate the gospel message.

_____ yes   _____ no

Things to Do

☐ _Find a solid Bible study, such as those offered by the Bereans at www.bbsg.org and its related links, that will deepen your knowledge of God and His Word._

☐ _Use the Internet to research a subject you are curious about._

☐ _Learn all aspects of a current political issue so that you can intellectually defend your position._

☐ _Read an article or book by an apologist like Josh McDowell on how you can intellectually defend your faith._

☐ _Thank God for the intelligence He has given you._

☐ _Consciously set the Holy Spirit as a guard over your mind and trust Him to lead you into truth._

Things to Remember

A house is built by wisdom and becomes strong through good sense.

PROVERBS 24:3 NLT

[Paul wrote,] Because of God's gracious gift to me I say to every one of you: Do not think of yourself more highly than you should. Instead, be modest in your thinking, and judge yourself according to the amount of faith God has given you.

ROMANS 12:3 GNT

Some [Christians] are accustomed to thinking of idols as being real, so when they eat food that has been offered to idols, they think of it as the worship of real gods, and their weak consciences are violated.

1 CORINTHIANS 8:7 NLT

[Paul wrote,] Remember how you were when you didn't know God, led from one phony god to another, never knowing what you were doing, just doing it because everybody else did it? It's different in this life. God wants us to use our intelligence, to seek to understand as well as we can.

1 CORINTHIANS 12:2 THE MESSAGE

God does not require you to follow His leadings on blind trust. Behold the evidence of an invisible intelligence pervading everything, even your own mind and body.

RAYMOND HOLLIWELL

Intelligence must follow faith, never precede it, and never destroy it.

THOMAS À KEMPIS

Conformity

Assembly Line

Do not be conformed to this world, but be transformed by the renewing of your mind, that you may prove what is that good and acceptable and perfect will of God.

ROMANS 12:2 NKJV

The four young men had been lifelong friends, joined by their common status as foreigners in the country in which they now lived. Here, the laws were different from the ones back home—so different, in fact, that these four teenagers could not follow them with a clear conscience. They had no choice; they had to defy the most powerful man in the country, who happened also to be the cruelest man in the country, and maybe even in the world. Their future did not exactly look promising.

The four youths—Shadrach, Meshach, Abednego, and Daniel—refused to conform to certain customs of the Babylonian world in which they lived, one of which included obeying King Nebuchadnezzar's every decree. It was the king who had insisted that the four friends feast on meat and wine, thinking such a diet would ensure that they would become the strong and robust men he needed in his service. But the youths were Jews, and for them it was against the laws of God to eat meat that had been offered to idols. How could they be certain the meat had not been offered to idols? They couldn't, and so they obtained permission to follow an alternative plan from a lesser official with whom they had found favor: They would eat only vegetables and drink only water for a period of ten days. When their experiment ended ten days later, the four friends were found to be healthier than those in the palace who had feasted on the meat and wine of the royal diet. God had honored their commitment to following His laws.

Daniel and his friends, who are believed to have been about fourteen when this incident occurred, were clearly a group of nonconformists in their day and time. At such a young age, they probably would have been forgiven had they been intimidated into following the king's dietary orders. Yet look at how they handled the situation despite their age: They courageously refused to follow a royal decree that conflicted with their faith, but they did so by providing a creative solution, which they presented in a respectful way.

Hundreds of years later, the apostle Paul would write a letter to the church in Rome that included one sentence summing up the way believers should operate in an unbelieving environment: "Do not be conformed to this world, but be transformed by the renewing of your mind, that you may prove what is that good and acceptable and perfect will of God" (Romans 12:2 NKJV). Sounds exactly like what Daniel and his friends did, doesn't it? Daniel's renewed mind provided a creative solution that did in fact prove what God's will was for him and his friends.

As you discover a new level of freedom in your life, you may find yourself tempted to throw off the conventions of the culture around you. But refusing to conform to the standards of society simply for the sake of being a nonconformist is not the point of Paul's admonition; those who follow that path merely end up conforming to the standards of the nonconformists. Paul is warning against conformity to the world's standards of faith and morality when they conflict with the biblical standards of faith and morality. The power to defy the world's standards comes when you offer yourself to the Lord to allow Him to transform you. You become transformed when you renew your mind—exchanging your old mind, with its worldly pattern of thinking, for the mind of Christ.

Your renewed mind accomplishes a great deal, not the least of which is the ability to tactfully and graciously refuse to conform. Like Daniel and his friends, you can defy the "king's decrees" in ways that are respectful and creative. Unless and until God directs you to do otherwise, you would be wise to follow that model of behavior; your gentle approach may prove to carry far more influence and weight than a hostile act of defiance ever could.

Take Paul's words to heart. Trust God to give you the courage to refuse to conform to the moral standards of the world around you; learn to live solely in conformity to biblical standards. Offer your worldly mind in exchange for the mind of Christ.

I Will

Count on God to give me the courage to resist
conforming to the world's standards.

yes _____ _no_ _____

Be transformed by the renewing of my mind.

yes _____ _no_ _____

Believe that I can have the mind of Christ.

yes _____ _no_ _____

Realize that nonconformity is not the point;
conforming to God's standards is.

yes _____ _no_ _____

Maintain a respectful attitude toward those whose
standards differ from mine.

yes _____ _no_ _____

Trust God to give me creative solutions to the
problems I can expect to encounter.

yes _____ _no_ _____

Things to Do

☐ _Read the story of the four friends in Daniel 1._

☐ _Memorize Romans 12:2._

☐ _Meditate on what it means to be transformed by the renewing of
your mind._

☐ _Read the quotations at the end of this devotional and then come up
with your own quotation about conformity._

☐ _Read about the life of Martin Luther, whose unconventional
interpretation of Scripture helped reform the church._

☐ _Make a mutual commitment with a friend to help each other resist
conforming to the world's standards of faith and morality._

☐ _Pray to God for the ability to remain gracious and respectful._

Things to Remember

[Ezekiel told the Israelites,] "Therefore this is what the Sovereign LORD says: You have been more unruly than the nations around you and have not followed my decrees or kept my laws. You have not even conformed to the standards of the nations around you."

EZEKIEL 5:7 NIV

Those God foreknew he also predestined to be conformed to the likeness of his Son, that he might be the firstborn among many brothers.

ROMANS 8:29 NIV

[Paul wrote,] If we live by our spiritual nature, then our lives need to conform to our spiritual nature.

Galatians 5:25 GOD'S WORD

As obedient children, do not conform to the evil desires you had when you lived in ignorance.

1 PETER 1:14 NIV

Those of Israelite descent had separated themselves from all foreigners. They stood in their places and confessed their sins and the wickedness of their fathers. They stood where they were and read from the Book of the Law of the LORD their God for a quarter of the day, and spent another quarter in confession and in worshiping the LORD their God.

NEHEMIAH 9:2–3 NIV

[Paul wrote,] What agreement is there between the temple of God and idols? For we are the temple of the living God. As God has said: "I will live with them and walk among them, and I will be their God, and they will be my people. Therefore come out from them and be separate, says the Lord. Touch no unclean thing, and I will receive you."

2 CORINTHIANS 6:16–17 NIV

[The Lord said,] "Obey my laws, and live by them. I am the LORD who sets you apart as holy."

LEVITICUS 20:8 GOD'S WORD

[Solomon wrote,] My son, if sinners entice you, do not give in to them.

PROVERBS 1:10 NIV

[God said to the Israelites,] "I will make my home among them. I will be their God, and they will be my people. And since my Temple will remain among them forever, the nations will know that I, the LORD, have set Israel apart for myself to be holy."

EZEKIEL 37:27–28 NLT

It is said that if Noah's ark had to be built by a company; they would not have laid the keel yet; and it may be so. What is many men's business is nobody's business. The greatest things are accomplished by individual men.

CHARLES HADDON SPURGEON

Conformity is the jailer of freedom and the enemy of growth.

JOHN F. KENNEDY

Leadership

Setting an Example

[Paul wrote to Timothy,] Let no one despise your youth, but be an example to the believers in word, in conduct, in love, in spirit, in faith, in purity.

1 TIMOTHY 4:12 NKJV

What picture comes to your mind when the word *leadership* is mentioned? Do you see those of your peers who were involved in student government? Or maybe you think of the president of the United States or a Christian like John Maxwell, who has dedicated his ministry to training others—including young people—to assume positions of leadership in the church and in society.

All of those are valid depictions of leadership, but there is a sense in which every believer is a leader, and that is in the concept of servant leadership. Throughout your postgraduation life, you will be called on to lead others even if you are not a leader by nature. One common example of this will be evident the day you become a parent for the first time. Suddenly, you are being called upon to direct a child in a way of life that will lead him or her to faith in Christ. How will you respond to the call to leadership?

Whether your call involves leading a corporation of 10,000 employees or a family of three, one of the principles of leadership that will always apply to you is the concept of servant leadership—leading others by serving them. This biblical concept runs counter to the kind of leadership you are likely to find in an aggressively competitive secular environment. There you may meet people who consider the notion of serving others to be laughable, but God knows that the best leaders are those whose actions flow from a heart full of love and humility toward others.

In a practical sense servant leadership involves setting an example. Former President Jimmy Carter—at one time the most powerful man in the world—does this regularly as he helps build houses for the underprivileged through the ministry of Habitat for Humanity. That's servant leadership at work: using your visible position as a leader to serve people, thereby inspiring others to do the same. In the context of your eventual role as a parent, for example, that will mean serving your spouse and setting an example of a godly marriage for your children. In the near future it may mean taking out the trash as your roommates bicker over whose turn it is.

Servant leadership is what the incarnation of Jesus Christ is all about: God humbling Himself by coming to Earth and serving humanity by sacrificing Himself in our place. Keep that prime example in mind whenever you are called upon to be a leader of others.

I Will

Lead others by serving them. ___yes___ ___no___

Learn from the example of the ultimate servant leader, Jesus Christ. ___yes___ ___no___

Maintain an attitude of love and humility toward those I am called to lead. ___yes___ ___no___

Recognize the leadership roles I am called to take on even if I do not consider myself a born leader. ___yes___ ___no___

Seek to inspire others by setting a good example. ___yes___ ___no___

Trust God to give me the ability to lead others when I am called on to do so. ___yes___ ___no___

Things to Do

☐ Ask your pastor or youth leader to recommend leadership training materials appropriate for your age group.

☐ Read the Gospel of John and note the ways in which Jesus exemplified the concept of servant leadership.

☐ Try to find an example of a servant leader in your community.

☐ Memorize 1 Timothy 4:12.

☐ Come up with at least one practical way you can demonstrate servant leadership in your own life right now.

☐ Ask God to give you a heart full of love and humility toward those you serve through leadership.

Things to Remember

[Paul wrote,] In everything set [young men] an example by doing what is good. In your teaching show integrity, seriousness and soundness of speech that cannot be condemned, so that those who oppose you may be ashamed because they have nothing bad to say about us.

TITUS 2:7–8 NIV

[Paul wrote,] Dear brothers, pattern your lives after mine, and notice who else lives up to my example.

PHILIPPIANS 3:17 TLB

[Paul wrote to Timothy,] Here is a saying you can trust. If anyone wants to be a leader in the church, he wants to do a good work for God and people.

1 TIMOTHY 3:1 NIrV

Take up the whole armor of God, that you may be able to withstand in the evil day, and having done all, to stand.

EPHESIANS 6:13 NKJV

[Paul wrote] Imitate me, just as I also imitate Christ.

1 CORINTHIANS 11:1 NKJV

A good leader takes a little more than his share of the blame, a little less than his share of the credit.

ARNOLD H. GLASGOW

A leader is one who knows the way, goes the way and shows the way.

JOHN C. MAXWELL

Love

Guarding Your Heart

Watch over your heart with all diligence, for from it flow the springs of life.

Proverbs 4:23 NASB

How do you know if you're really in love? Throughout your life, you've seen real-life and cinematic glimpses of what love is supposed to look like, but still you're confused—especially if you've had several relationships in which you thought you had found the real thing. Instead, you were left with doubt and frustration, or worst of all, a broken heart. Now, as you stand on the brink of a future that you expect will include marriage, you may wonder more than ever if genuine love is even a reality.

You can protect your heart from future hurt and keep yourself open to the possibility of true love by learning what genuine love is—from the One who is love and who created human beings to love each other. By His definition—the only one that counts, by the way—true love is unconditional.

What does that mean for you? It means that your love for another is not contingent on what that person does for you, like making you feel good, or on that person's external characteristics, like his or her appearance. Feelings that are dependent on changeable qualities like those are fickle; when the person no longer makes you feel good or no longer looks the same, will your feelings change?

Unconditional love is love *no matter what*—love in spite of who or what a person is. It's love in spite of both the good and the bad; it's love that cannot be earned, cannot be changed, and cannot be lost. It's the kind of love with which God loves you.

Genuine love is also based on giving, not getting, and that one aspect can often serve as a litmus test of true love. Do you want to give to another person—or do you mostly just want to get? Love that wants to give and keep on giving, with no thought of reward, is love that is likely to last.

First Corinthians 13 says it best: Genuine love, the love God wants us to have for others, is patient, kind, eternal. It's never selfish or jealous or boastful or proud or demanding. Genuine love serves the needs of the one who is loved.

Guard your heart against the pain of broken relationships by refusing to settle for anything less than the true and unconditional love described in the Bible. That's the kind of love God has for you—and as always, His is the best example to follow.

I Will

Realize that true love comes with no strings attached.

yes ___ _no_ ___

Focus on giving rather than receiving in a love relationship.

yes ___ _no_ ___

Refuse to settle for anything less than the kind of love described in 1 Corinthians 13.

yes ___ _no_ ___

Be continually thankful to God for His unconditional love for me.

yes ___ _no_ ___

Guard my heart against the pain that comes with false love relationships.

yes ___ _no_ ___

Learn to be patient and wait for the right person to come along.

yes ___ _no_ ___

Things to Do

☐ _Read 1 Corinthians 13 and memorize verses 4–7._

☐ _Watch a current romantic movie and determine if the love between the principal characters is unconditional._

☐ _Read the story of Jacob's love for Rachel in Genesis 29, making note of all that he agreed to do in order to marry her._

☐ _Ask God to help you as you work on qualities essential to a love relationship, such as patience and kindness._

☐ _Pray for your future mate, even though you probably don't know who that is yet._

☐ _Using an online search engine, do a study of the word love as it is used in the Bible._

Things to Remember

Love is patient. Love is kind. It does not want what belongs to others. It does not brag. It is not proud.

1 CORINTHIANS 13:4 NIrV

Love is eternal. There are inspired messages, but they are temporary; there are gifts of speaking in strange tongues, but they will cease; there is knowledge, but it will pass.

1 CORINTHIANS 13:8 GNT

[John wrote,] We have known and believed the love that God has for us. God is love.

1 JOHN 4:16 NKJV

Owe no one anything except to love one another.

ROMANS 13:8 NKJV

The three most important things to have are faith, hope and love. But the greatest of them is love.

1 CORINTHIANS 13:13 NIrV

I never knew how to worship until I knew how to love.
HENRY WARD BEECHER

You will find, as you look back upon your life, that the moments when you really lived are the moments when you have done things in the spirit of love.

HENRY DRUMMOND

Calling

Is That You, God?

I know the thoughts that I think toward you, says the Lord, thoughts of peace and not of evil, to give you a future and a hope.

JEREMIAH 29:11 NKJV

From the time she was a child, Carissa wanted to be a teacher. That's not so unusual, of course; lots of young children look up to their teachers and want to be like them when they grow up. Eventually, most students begin to look elsewhere for their career role models. But not Carissa. She knew, way down deep inside, that she was meant to be a teacher. This was her calling—the life choice God wanted her to make, confirmed through prayer and the counsel of her parents and other adults.

Over four years of college, though, Carissa began to have her doubts. It started when her suite mates in the dorm kept asking her why on Earth she would ever want to be a teacher when she could make *real* money in the business world. Teaching? No thanks. They'd rather take a stab at a profession that at least held out the hope of a six-figure salary one day.

Then there were the conflicts in every school she visited. Several teachers took her aside and told her what teaching was *really* like: the politics, excessive paperwork, backstabbing colleagues, complaining parents, violent students. Determined to look past the negatives, Carissa kept her focus on her goal. But the clincher came during her student-teaching experience; standing in front of a room full of fifth-graders, she felt as if she didn't belong there. What was going on?

Carissa talked out her doubts with several counselors who asked her lots of questions—about the motives of those who tried to discourage her, about the certainty of her original sense of calling, about the wisdom of pursuing a high salary over her heart's desire, and so forth. Today, Carissa is thriving in her profession—but she is not the classroom teacher she thought she would be. Instead, she works for a nonprofit agency, training volunteers for international relief work.

Through the counseling she received, Carissa realized that teaching was her calling, but her calling was much bigger than she originally thought. She learned that her calling as a teacher transcended any one specific job. Throughout the course of her life, Carissa may fulfill her calling in any number of settings: as a corporate trainer, as a missionary, as a curriculum developer, as a Sunday school teacher, as a homeschooling mother, even as a traditional classroom teacher, at some other time. The important thing is that she is doing what she was meant to do, and that has made all the difference not only in her life but also in the lives of those around her.

In one sense that's what a calling is all about—making a difference. It's a deep desire to do something that drives you, something God has placed inside of you not only for your benefit but also for the benefit of others. All Christians have a general calling, the calling to be saints (see Romans 1:7). But you are also called to fulfill a special niche in this life, a unique purpose that's tailor-made for you.

Never make the mistake that many believers make—the mistake of thinking that the only people who are called by God are those who become pastors and other workers in full-time Christian ministry. Christians can make a difference in every area of life, and God calls His people to fulfill His purposes in a multitude of ways. While some believers can point to a specific moment in time when they knew what their calling was, most discover their calling over a period of time, through much prayer and counseling and self-examination.

Pay close attention to what it is that drives you, the talents you possess, the experiences you have had, the things that make you feel alive. Ask God to show you what He has called you to do. Talk out your thoughts and dreams and desires with adults you trust. Don't miss out on fulfilling your calling by settling for second-best, no matter how attractive second-best appears to be. Accept nothing but the very best, the life God has called you to live. Like Carissa, you could make a difference in the lives of others—and your decision will certainly make all the difference in your own life.

I Will

Believe that God has a specific calling for me. _yes_ _no_

Understand that a calling does not necessarily mean full-time Christian work. _yes_ _no_

Expect God to confirm that what I believe is my calling is actually what He has for me. _yes_ _no_

Believe that I can make a difference in the people around me, no matter what I am called to do. _yes_ _no_

Accept the counsel of those whose wisdom I value. _yes_ _no_

Keep my focus on God's purpose for my life rather than the perks of a career. _yes_ _no_

Things to Do

☐ List your talents and skills, along with those things that you are most passionate about.

☐ Give the list to God and ask Him to show you how the items on it may reveal your ultimate calling.

☐ Find at least two adults who may be able to help you determine your calling.

☐ Look for resources to help determine your calling, such as Patrick Morley's "Twelve Suggestions to Help Discover Your Calling" (http://www.maninthemirror.org/alm/alm6.htm; the principles apply to females as well).

☐ Write in your journal about how you could make a difference in the career you've been planning to pursue.

☐ Memorize 2 Peter 1:3 or another verse from the following pages.

Things to Remember

The LORD came and stood there, calling as at the other times, "Samuel! Samuel!" Then Samuel said, "Speak, for your servant is listening."

1 SAMUEL 3:10 NIV

As Jesus was walking beside the Sea of Galilee, he saw two brothers, Simon called Peter and his brother Andrew. They were casting a net into the lake, for they were fishermen. "Come, follow me," Jesus said, "and I will make you fishers of men."

MATTHEW 4:18–19 NIV

[Paul wrote,] As a prisoner for the Lord, then, I urge you to live a life worthy of the calling you have received.
Ephesians 4:1 NIV

From the standpoint of the gospel [the Jews] are enemies for your sake, but from the standpoint of God's choice they are beloved for the sake of the fathers; for the gifts and the calling of God are irrevocable.

ROMANS 11:28–29 NASB

[Jesus] saw a man named Matthew sitting at the tax collector's booth. "Follow me," he told him, and Matthew got up and followed him.

MATTHEW 9:9 NIV

His divine power has given us everything we need for life and godliness through our knowledge of him who called us by his own glory and goodness.

2 PETER 1:3 NIV

[Paul wrote,] I pray that the eyes of your heart may be enlightened, so that you will know what is the hope of His calling, what are the riches of the glory of His inheritance in the saints.

EPHESIANS 1:18 NASB

My Christian friends, who also have been called by God! Think of Jesus, whom God sent to be the High Priest of the faith we profess.

HEBREWS 3:1 GNT

[Peter wrote,] Dear brothers and sisters, work hard to prove that you really are among those God has called and chosen. Doing this, you will never stumble or fall away.

2 PETER 1:10 NLT

[Paul wrote,] We constantly pray for you, that our God may count you worthy of his calling, and that by his power he may fulfill every good purpose of yours and every act prompted by your faith.

2 THESSALONIANS 1:11 NIV

To hunger for use and to go unused is the worst hunger of all.

LYNDON B. JOHNSON

Every calling is great when greatly pursued.

OLIVER WENDELL HOLMES

Maturity

Prime of Life

Leaving the discussion of the elementary principles of Christ, let us go on to perfection, not laying again the foundation of repentance from dead works and of faith toward God.

HEBREWS 6:1 NKJV

Now that you've reached this significant milestone in your life—graduation—you probably realize something that you've long suspected: Age has little to do with maturity. In your own circle of friends, it's likely that you've sensed a fairly significant disparity in the maturity levels evident in the members of the group. It's also entirely possible that you are already more mature than people you know who are five or even ten older than you.

What accounts for the wildly varying levels of maturity you see in the people around you? Why aren't all twenty-year-olds equally mature—or at least somewhat alike in that regard? Part of the reason is that some people learn life's lessons more quickly than others do. They've learned from the example of others and from their own mistakes. Those who understand maturity best are likely to be those who have learned to draw on the wisdom of God.

If you were to ask ten people to list the top qualities of a mature person, you'd probably receive ten different responses. But there are certain characteristics that few would argue with; if you want to gauge where you stand on the road to maturity, you might want to start by examining these qualities in your life:

A mature person exhibits self-control. Lack of self-control is a mark of immaturity. Learn to control your thoughts, actions, temper, tongue, desires, passions—all of those things that war against your godly nature—and you'll find yourself farther down the road than you could ever imagine.

A mature person is other-centered, not self-centered. Does your life revolve around you and your needs? Or have you learned to give equal attention to the needs of others? The Bible says you should love your neighbor as yourself, and that's impossible to do if your focus is entirely on yourself. Surrendering your needs and desires in order to meet the needs and desires of others is an integral part of growing up.

Finally, a mature person is a person of integrity—honest and trustworthy and aboveboard in all his dealings with other people. That means without exception; you can't cheat on your taxes and claim to be a person of integrity.

How do you measure up? As you rely on God to help you maintain self-control, focus on others, and become a person of integrity, you can be assured that you have what it takes to become a true grown-up.

I Will

Continually draw on the wisdom of God.

yes   no

Apply the lessons I learn from my mistakes and the mistakes of others.

yes   no

Understand that maturity is a process that includes changes in my character.

yes   no

Learn to control those aspects of my character that are natural enemies of my godly nature.

yes   no

Center my life on Christ and focus on meeting the needs of others.

yes   no

Become a person of integrity.

yes   no

Things to Do

- [ ] *List some characteristics of maturity other than the ones mentioned in the devotional.*

- [ ] *Engage your friends in a discussion about maturity—what the word means to them and how they gauge a person's maturity level.*

- [ ] *Ask God to reveal to you the areas of your life you need to work on to become more mature.*

- [ ] *Write in your journal about your own efforts at becoming more self-controlled.*

- [ ] *Decide once and for all that you will always strive to live a Christ-centered life.*

Things to Remember

Brethren, do not be children in understanding; however, in malice be babes, but in understanding be mature.

1 CORINTHIANS 14:20 NKJV

Anyone who lives on milk is still a baby. That person does not want to learn about living a godly life. Solid food is for those who are grown up. They have trained themselves with a lot of practice. They can tell the difference between good and evil.

HEBREWS 5:13–14 NIrV

[Paul wrote,] We preach Christ to everyone. With all possible wisdom we warn and teach them in order to bring each one into God's presence as a mature individual in union with Christ.

COLOSSIANS 1:28 GNT

Each of you should put your own actions to the test. Then you can take pride in yourself. You won't be comparing yourself to somebody else. Each of you should carry your own load.

GALATIANS 6:4–5 NIrV

Maturity: Be able to stick with a job until it is finished. Be able to bear an injustice without having to get even. Be able to carry money without spending it. Do your duty without being supervised.

ANN LANDERS

Maturity begins to grow when you can sense your concern for others outweighing your concern for yourself.

JOHN MACNAUGHTON

Mentors

Life Coach

As iron sharpens iron, so people can improve each other.

PROVERBS 27:17 NCV

If you've ever been involved in a sport, you're familiar with both the role and value of a coach. A good coach has a thorough understanding of the game and how it's played, a handle on your strengths and weaknesses and how they can be used to your advantage, and the patience and ability to train you to be better than you ever thought you could be. But when the game starts, you're the one who takes the field as your coach stands on the sidelines, encouraging, analyzing, and waiting to give you further instructions.

A life coach—a mentor—functions in much the same way. Finding mentors for your future career and your spiritual life is one of the smartest actions you can take to give you a strong start in life. Finding a single mentor who can coach you in both fields at once is a double blessing, giving you the assurance that the career guidance you receive will line up with the biblical principles you strive to live by.

Where can you find this awesome person? There's a good chance you already know someone who would be willing to take you under his or her wing. Look around your church, your campus, or your parents' circle of friends. Is there someone you feel relaxed with, someone of integrity who has shown a personal interest in your life? Ask him if you could spend some time with him, observing him as he goes about his routine. Ask her if she would be willing to teach you about her career field. Above all, ask them if they would walk alongside you as you attempt to live out a life of faith during this new phase of your life.

What should you look for in a mentor? Look for a godly person, first of all. Find someone you can be yourself with, someone you can discuss difficult and personal issues with. Seek out a person who accepts you as you are, who listens attentively to you, who encourages you and corrects you in a spirit of love.

Remember: You are responsible for being a respectful apprentice. Return your mentor's favors by being respectful of his time, listening just as attentively to her as she listens to you, following his advice, showing up on time, acknowledging her impact on your life. Pray for your mentor and the mentoring relationship you've established. Mentoring offers a priceless opportunity to help you get started in life; treat the experience with a corresponding degree of appreciation.

I Will

Acknowledge the importance of learning from someone more experienced than I am.

_____ yes   _____ no

Place a high priority on finding a spiritual mentor.

_____ yes   _____ no

Trust God to lead me to the right life coach.

_____ yes   _____ no

Respect my mentor's time and counsel.

_____ yes   _____ no

Be a good listener.

_____ yes   _____ no

Be open and transparent with my life coach.

_____ yes   _____ no

Learn how to mentor someone else by observing my own mentor.

_____ yes   _____ no

Things to Do

☐ *Find an older person who is willing to walk alongside you on your faith journey.*

☐ *List the qualities a person would need to exhibit in order to be an appropriate mentor for you.*

☐ *Clearly define your career goals and seek out a mentor whose current career path reflects your goals.*

☐ *Pray that God will show you how to approach a prospective life coach when asking him to mentor you.*

☐ *Ask God to point out any blind spots you may have as an apprentice.*

☐ *Journal about your experience in finding and working with a mentor.*

Things to Remember

If you instruct the brethren in [spiritual] things, you will be a good minister of Jesus Christ, nourished in the words of faith.

1 TIMOTHY 4:6 NKJV

Do not want what evil men have. Don't long to be with them.

PROVERBS 24:1 NIrV

When the boy Samuel was serving the LORD under the direction of Eli, there were very few messages from the LORD, and visions from him were quite rare.

1 SAMUEL 3:1 GNT

"Come. Follow me," Jesus said. "I will make you fishers of people."

MATTHEW 4:19 NIrV

Jesus took with him Peter, James, and John, and led them up a high mountain, where they were alone. As they looked on, a change came over Jesus.

MARK 9:2 GNT

Mentoring is all about people—it's about caring, about relationships and sensitivity.

RENE CARAYOL

My chief want in life is someone who shall make me do what I can.

RALPH WALDO EMERSON

Mission Statement

True North

"Thus speaks the LORD God of Israel, saying: 'Write in a book for yourself all the words that I have spoken to you.'"

JEREMIAH 30:2 NKJV

In the 1996 movie *Jerry Maguire,* the title character handles disillusionment with his job by spending all night writing a mission statement. The result is a twenty-seven-page document describing the values Maguire held when he began his career as a sports attorney and the loss of those values as he and the firm he works for became consumed with their success. Maguire ends his mission statement where his career began, with his desire to live and die for a cause—the cause of "caring about each other."

As a new graduate you have a clear advantage over Maguire, who needed to reach a crisis point before he realized how far he had strayed from the person he intended to be. You can avoid wasting years of your life—and watching your values erode—by writing a personal mission statement now, before your career gets in the way.

Just what is a mission statement? First off, it's generally not a twenty-seven-page document. It can be as short as a paragraph or as long as you want it to be. The important thing is that it defines your hopes and dreams for the kind of person you want to be and the kind of life you want to have. It's all about what's important to you, what really matters when you strip away all the inconsequential details of life.

You can write your own mission statement by simply answering a few basic questions. Here are a few:

What do you want your life to be about? As a believer you most likely would want your life to be about your relationships—first with God, and then with others. You need to answer that question for yourself, as honestly and completely as you can.

What do you want to live for? What—if anything—are you willing to die for? Think this through carefully, because your answers to these questions define exactly what your life stands for and what your values are.

What are you doing now to live the kind of life you wrote about in your previous answers? There's no need to wait until some indefinite time when you're older. If you're alive, you can start living in harmony with your mission statement right now.

The words you write can be a powerful force as long as you use them as a guiding light in your life. By regularly reviewing your mission statement, you keep reminding yourself of those things that Maguire lost sight of—the things that really matter.

I Will

Define my values and keep them in mind.   yes ____ no ____

Rely on God as I determine what my values are.   yes ____ no ____

Realize that my priority needs to be my
relationships with God and others.   yes ____ no ____

Begin living in harmony with my mission statement. yes ____ no ____

Be honest with myself as I begin to examine what
my life is about.   yes ____ no ____

Regularly review my mission statement.   yes ____ no ____

Trust God to help me maintain my values and
standards throughout my life.   yes ____ no ____

Things to Do

☐ Ask God to help you as you begin to write your personal mission statement.

☐ Find mission statements on the Internet to use as examples.

☐ Ask around to see if you can find an adult who has written a mission statement and is willing to help you.

☐ Answer the questions on the preceding page to begin writing your mission statement.

☐ Post your completed statement in a prominent place in your room.

☐ Schedule a time—say, six months or a year from now—to prayerfully review and possibly revise your statement.

Things to Remember

[Paul wrote,] In Him also we have obtained an inheritance, being predestined according to the purpose of Him who works all things according to the counsel of His will, that we who first trusted in Christ should be to the praise of His glory.

EPHESIANS 1:11–12 NKJV

God is at work with you, helping you want to obey him, and then helping you do what he wants.

PHILIPPIANS 2:13 TLB

[Paul wrote,] God planned for us to do good things and to live as he has always wanted us to live. That's why he sent Christ to make us what we are.

EPHESIANS 2:10 CEV

[Jesus said,] "Let your light shine in front of others. Then they will see the good things you do. And they will praise your Father who is in heaven."

MATTHEW 5:16 NIrV

What you should say is this: "If the Lord is willing, we will live and do this or that."

JAMES 4:15 GNT

Above all be of single aim; have a legitimate and useful purpose, and devote yourself unreservedly to it.

JAMES ALLEN

Existence is a strange bargain. Life owes us little; we owe it everything. The only true happiness comes from squandering ourselves for a purpose.

WILLIAM COWPER

Respect

Regard for Authority

[The Lord said,] "Show respect to old people; stand up in their presence. Show respect also to your God. I am the LORD."

LEVITICUS 19:32 NCV

Now that you're entering this new phase of your life, you may feel that you can breathe a sigh of relief: "Finally. Now I can make my own decisions, and no one can tell me what to do." You've got the first part right but not the second. Yes, you will be making more decisions on your own—but if you think no one can tell you what to do anymore, well, you need to remember all those people who are still authority figures in your life. Granted, only a few, such as a boss or a police officer, have the right to "tell" you what to do. Others, such as your pastor or a college professor, may only be in a position to advise you, but they still hold a position of authority in your life.

Your response to authority, of course, is all your own doing. Verses like 1 Peter 2:17 and others show you how God wants you to respond to the authorities He has placed over you; in short, He wants you to treat them with respect. Does that mean blindly following all that they tell you or advise you to do? Absolutely not, especially when their instructions to you conflict with Scripture or with what God has led you to do. But it does mean maintaining a respectful attitude toward those in authority even when you disagree with them.

Think of those in authority over your life as widening circles with you at the center. The first circle closest to you would be your parents or guardians. For some graduation signals a time of separation from family; if that's the case for you—if you will be moving away from home in the near future—you will still be able to honor your parents' authority by living a life that would be pleasing to them and respecting the values they taught you.

The next circle would include those who have direct authority over a specific aspect of your life, such as a boss, professor, or military officer—even a landlord, with regard to your living arrangement. That circle would also include a pastor or youth leader, who has the privilege of providing spiritual care for you. Finally, three outer circles encompass local, state, and national governments, with all their laws and enforcement agencies, especially if you travel, work, or study abroad.

Obviously, your obligations to each of those levels of authority vary widely, but God wants and expects you to show respect to each one. That desire and expectation applies whether or not you agree with those in authority over you. You may not like a law the state legislature just passed, but you still have to show respect by obeying it. You may think your history professor's opinion on the relevance of the United Nations is misinformed, but you can disagree with her in a respectful way. You may secretly loathe your drill sergeant—he would have it no other way—but God still wants you to respect him (and even learn to love him).

It's not always easy to obey those who have authority over you. But it becomes easier when you recognize the authority of the One who is in authority over everyone. By recognizing that God has authority over your parents and the officer with the radar gun and a congressional delegation with the power to declare war, you realize that ultimately, the honor you show the authorities in your life is honor that you also show to God. That also makes you more aware of the need to pray for those authorities, that they would recognize God's authority and seek to make decisions in accordance with His will.

Honor God by honoring other people in your life. Be patient with those you disagree with. Be thankful that God has provided so many layers of protection for you. Acknowledge how difficult your life would be if you did not have all those authority figures looking out for you. Most important, be an example of godly behavior by treating other people with the kind of respect that will be a witness to the work of God in your life.

I Will

Respect the authority of others whether I agree with them or not.

yes   *no*

Willingly place myself under the spiritual authority of a respected Christian leader.

yes   *no*

Recognize the authority God has over me.

yes   *no*

Realize that showing respect to others is a sign of maturity.

yes   *no*

Understand that I will be under the authority of others throughout my life.

yes   *no*

Learn to adjust to new authorities in my life.

yes   *no*

Things to Do

☐ *List the authorities in your life—in your family, church, workplace, and community—and pray for them.*

☐ *Memorize one or more of the Bible verses in this section.*

☐ *Think of ways you can show respect to your boss or another authority figure in your life.*

☐ *Thank God for placing you under the authority of others.*

☐ *Thank your church pastor or youth pastor for the leadership he or she provides.*

☐ *Come up with three ways you can creatively show your parents you honor them.*

☐ *Ask God to give you patience with any authority figures you find it difficult to honor.*

Things to Remember

[Paul wrote,] Receive [Epaphroditus] with joy, as a believer in the Lord. Show respect to all such people as he.

PHILIPPIANS 2:29 GNT

[Paul wrote,] We beg you, our friends, to pay proper respect to those who work among you, who guide and instruct you in the Christian life. Treat them with the greatest respect and love because of the work they do. Be at peace among yourselves.

1 THESSALONIANS 5:12–13 GNT

> *Show proper respect to everyone. Love the community of believers. Have respect for God. Honor the king.*
> 1 Peter 2:17 NIrV

Obey your leaders, and accept their authority. They take care of you because they are responsible for you. Obey them so that they may do this work joyfully and not complain about you. (Causing them to complain would not be to your advantage.)

HEBREWS 13:17 GOD'S WORD

Fear of the LORD teaches a person to be wise; humility precedes honor.

PROVERBS 15:33 NLT

Pay [the authorities] what you owe them; pay them your personal and property taxes, and show respect and honor for them all.

ROMANS 13:7 GNT

Do not brag about yourself in front of a king or stand in the spot that belongs to notable people.

PROVERBS 25:6 GOD'S WORD

Whoever resists authority has opposed the ordinance of God; and they who have opposed will receive condemnation upon themselves.

ROMANS 13:2 NASB

Do nothing out of selfish ambition or vain conceit, but in humility consider others better than yourselves. Each of you should look not only to your own interests, but also to the interests of others. Your attitude should be the same as that of Christ Jesus.

PHILIPPIANS 2:3–5 NIV

When you are invited, go and sit in the lowest place, so that your host will come to you and say, "Come on up, my friend, to a better place." This will bring you honor in the presence of all the other guests.

LUKE 14:10 GNT

He that cannot decidedly say, "No," when tempted to evil, is on the highway to ruin. He loses the respect even of those who would tempt him, and becomes but the pliant tool and victim of their evil designs.

JOEL HAWES

People who look down on other people don't end up being looked up to.

ROBERT HALF

Obedience

Under Authority

Whoever resists the authority resists the ordinance of God, and those who resist will bring judgment on themselves.

ROMANS 13:2 NKJV

Have you ever read about the Israelites' complicated relationship with God? It wasn't God who did the complicating. It was the Israelites, or more accurately, their disobedience that was responsible for the problems that existed between God and His chosen people. You have to wonder why they continued to disobey when He repeatedly promised to bless their obedience.

Just look at one passage in the Bible, Deuteronomy 28:2-8. He promised them so much. The reality is that He has also promised to bless your obedience to Him and to those He has placed in authority over you. That includes more people than you may realize. Now that you have graduated and are entering a new phase of adulthood, you may find it especially difficult to accept the fact that there are still areas of your life in which you must be obedient to others.

Most likely, you will have a number of people in authority over you for some time to come—professors, if you are continuing your education; officers, if you are entering military service; and bosses at the jobs you will hold. The extent of your obedience to those authorities, of course, is limited to their sphere of influence, such as the academic world or the military or the workplace. Likewise, God expects you to be obedient to the laws of the land, as long as they do not conflict with biblical principles. In no situation does God want you to obey a person or institutional authority that requires you to do anything contrary to the will and Word of God.

One special authority over you is your parents. Now that you are an adult, your relationship with them will understandably change. Are you still required to obey them? Yes and no. Certainly you need to obey their house rules if you still live with them or anytime you visit if you've moved out. Out of love and respect for them, you will no doubt want to maintain an attitude of obedience toward them. But as an adult, ultimately you are answerable to God alone for the decisions you make; you can't expect to go before God when you've made a bad decision and use the excuse, "My parents made me do it."

When you think about it, God asks very little of you. He wants you to be obedient to Him and to the authorities He has placed over you. That's really not so much to ask, considering all He has blessed you with.

I Will

Maintain an attitude of obedience toward God.   _yes_   _no_

Be thankful for God's promises to bless my obedience.   _yes_   _no_

Recognize the authorities God has placed over me.   _yes_   _no_

Continue to respond obediently to my parents, out of love and respect for them.   _yes_   _no_

Realize that my obedience to others ends when their directives conflict with God's will.   _yes_   _no_

Remember that ultimately, I am responsible for the decisions I make as an adult.   _yes_   _no_

Pray for those in authority over me.   _yes_   _no_

Things to Do

☐ *Memorize at least one of the Bible verses on the facing page.*

☐ *List the authorities in your life and think about how you could be more obedient to each one.*

☐ *In an online Bible encyclopedia, read a synopsis of the Israelites' relationship with God.*

☐ *Write in your journal about a time when God blessed you for your obedience.*

☐ *Read the account of Jesus' night of prayer in the Garden of Gethsemane in Matthew 26:36–46, noting His words of obedience.*

☐ *Go through your day tomorrow paying attention to all the opportunities you have to be obedient.*

Things to Remember

[Jesus said,] "If you obey my commands, you will remain in my love, just as I have obeyed my Father's commands and remain in his love."

JOHN 15:10 GNT

[Jesus said,] "Not everyone who says to me, 'Lord, Lord' will enter the kingdom of heaven, but he who does the will of my Father who is in heaven will enter."

MATTHEW 7:21 NASB

Obey your leaders and submit to their authority. They keep watch over you as men who must give an account. Obey them so that their work will be a joy, not a burden, for that would be of no advantage to you.

HEBREWS 13:17 NIV

Samuel said, "Has the LORD as much delight in burnt offerings and sacrifices as in obeying the voice of the LORD? Behold, to obey is better than sacrifice, and to heed than the fat of rams."

1 SAMUEL 15:22 NASB

[God said,] "Oh, that they had such a heart in them that they would fear Me and always keep all My commandments, that it might be well with them and with their children forever!"

DEUTERONOMY 5:29 NKJV

No principle is so noble, as there is none more holy, than that of a true obedience.

HENRY GILES

Every great person has first learned how to obey, whom to obey, and when to obey.

WILLIAM A. WARD

Perspective

Theory of Relativity

Beloved, do not forget this one thing, that with the Lord one day is as a thousand years, and a thousand years as one day.

2 PETER 3:8 NKJV

Three witnesses to an accident are questioned by the investigating police officer. Witness A was just coming out of a convenience store when he heard the collision and looked around a panel truck to see the aftermath. Witness B was crossing the street when the collision occurred and was so shaken by the incident that she blacked out and had to be treated for shock. Witness C was taking a break from work on a third-story balcony and witnessed the entire accident.

Which account are the police most likely to trust? The most complete account, right?

In a similar way you need to determine whom you can trust to help you interpret the events in your life, especially now that you are entering a new level of independence. Maybe you've had a falling out with a longtime friend. As far as you're concerned, your friend treated you badly, choosing to spend the weekend with his roommate's family instead of going to a Saturday football game with you, as the two of you had planned. The way your friend sees it, his plans with you were never definite, and he had promised to help his roommate's father set up a Web site. But there's a third perspective, a far more important one: God's. He knows what you don't: that this weekend, your friend will have a powerful encounter with Him at his roommate's house.

When you start to recognize that God's perspective may be entirely different from your own, you begin to relax and take things in stride. People who overreact when things don't go their way often do so because they think they understand the situation perfectly well. They fail to look at the incident from anyone else's perspective but their own—least of all, God's. All they actually see is a tiny, blurred portion of the big picture.

As long as you are alive on Earth, you will never be able to see the complete picture regarding any situation. That special view, that unique perspective, is reserved for God alone. He wants you to understand that and learn to take His perspective into consideration as you attempt to interpret the meaning behind the events in your life. Sometimes, He will offer you a glimpse into the situation as He sees it, but many times He will not. You will simply have to trust that He is involved behind the scenes, accomplishing much more than you may ever find out about.

I Will

Learn to take God's perspective into consideration. _yes_ _no_

Be sensitive to another person's perspective when
we disagree. _yes_ _no_

Trust that God is always involved behind the scenes. _yes_ _no_

Begin to take difficult or unpleasant situations in
stride. _yes_ _no_

Realize that all I will ever see is a tiny portion of
each incident in my life. _yes_ _no_

Give others the benefit of the doubt when I feel
they've wronged me. _yes_ _no_

Things to Do

☐ *Think about Jesus' crucifixion from the perspectives of God the Father,
Jesus, Jesus' followers, the Romans, and the Jewish religious leaders.*

☐ *Write out Isaiah 55:8 and post it where you will see it each day.*

☐ *Read the quotations about perspective on the facing page and try
writing a quotation of your own.*

☐ *Help a friend to see a current, difficult situation from a different
perspective.*

☐ *Ask God to open your eyes to the way He sees a current situation in
your own life.*

☐ *Read the book of Job for an eye-opening look at the disparity between
human and godly perspectives.*

Things to Remember

[Paul wrote,] We fix our attention, not on things that are seen, but on things that are unseen. What can be seen lasts only for a time, but what cannot be seen lasts forever.

2 CORINTHIANS 4:18 GNT

God looked over all he had made, and he saw that it was excellent in every way. This all happened on the sixth day.

GENESIS 1:31 NLT

[God said,] "My thoughts are not like your thoughts. And your ways are not like my ways."

ISAIAH 55:8 NIrV

[The psalmist wrote,] Open my eyes to see the wonderful truths in your law.

PSALM 119:18 NLT

[God said to Job,] "Were you there when I made the world? If you know so much, tell me about it."

JOB 38:4 GNT

If the only tool you have is a hammer, you tend to see every problem as a nail.

ABRAHAM H. MASLOW

The difference between a mountain and a molehill is your perspective.

AL NEUHARTH

Physical Well-Being

Healthy Choice

Don't be impressed with your own wisdom. Instead, fear the LORD and turn your back on evil. Then you will gain renewed health and vitality.

As a recent graduate you will face any number of temptations that could have an adverse effect on your well-being. Putting on some extra pounds is a possibility if you succumb to the temptation to eat out rather than to plan meals, grocery shop, and cook. But you can beat the odds and stay—or get—physically fit by combining a few biblical principles with a healthy lifestyle.

First, God created your body, and you honor Him by taking good care of it, through physical exercise, good nutrition, and the right amount of rest—all of those things you learned about in health class. Second, your body is the temple of God's Spirit, and when you keep yourself morally pure, you also honor God with your body. Finally, by keeping yourself physically fit, you keep yourself energetic and fit for service to God.

How can you incorporate healthy habits into your

new and suddenly independent lifestyle? Take a good look at each of the three areas of healthy living—exercise, diet, and rest—and decide what you could do to stay fit. For example, the word *exercise* may make you think of high school calisthenics, but it simply means moving your body more. Even if you're not in to sports—extreme or otherwise—you can take long walks with a friend or learn kick boxing in the privacy of your room. Just get moving.

Good nutrition often involves making decisions ahead of time. If you know your friends are heavily into chips and dip or nachos and cheese, prepare yourself by bringing along a more healthful snack, such as a bag of baby carrots, when you join them to watch some videos. Bring enough to share— you'll feel less awkward than you would if you only brought your own "diet" portion, and you may even start a trend among your friends.

Once you start to move more and eat less—or eat better— you'll probably find that getting the right amount of rest will take care of itself. The body God designed is wonderfully efficient; there's no need to place an inordinate amount of attention on your physical well-being.

Honor God by making the right choices and finding the right balance between your efforts to stay physically fit and all the other demands on your time. You can rely on God's wisdom to help you find that balance.

I Will

Honor God with my body.   *yes*   *no*

Remember that my body is the temple of the
Holy Spirit.   *yes*   *no*

Seek to achieve balance in my efforts to be
physically fit.   *yes*   *no*

Learn to make healthy decisions ahead of time—
before I'm faced with temptation.   *yes*   *no*

Be aware of the biblical principles that relate to
caring for the body.   *yes*   *no*

Desire to stay fit so I may have the energy and
well-being to serve God and others.   *yes*   *no*

Things to Do

☐ *Ask God to show you what you could be doing to get or stay in shape.*

☐ *Buy or borrow a good book on health for Christians, such as Kenneth Cooper's* Faith-Based Fitness *or Rex Russell's* What the Bible Says About Healthy Living.

☐ *Make a list of healthful foods you like—and use it when you go grocery shopping or out to eat.*

☐ *Come up with two or three kinds of exercise you like, and schedule them into your next week.*

☐ *Enlist a friend or two to help you stay properly focused on fitness.*

☐ *In your journal, write about how you're feeling physically at this time in your life; make a note to add a similar entry a month from now.*

Things to Remember

Do you not know that your body is a temple of the Holy Spirit, who is in you, whom you have received from God? You are not your own; you were bought at a price. Therefore honor God with your body.

1 CORINTHIANS 6:19–20 NIV

[John wrote,] Beloved, I pray that in all respects you may prosper and be in good health, just as your soul prospers.

3 JOHN 2 NASB

[Paul wrote,] My friends, because of God's great mercy to us I appeal to you: Offer yourselves as a living sacrifice to God, dedicated to his service and pleasing to him. This is the true worship that you should offer.

ROMANS 12:1 GNT

The LORD said to Samuel, "Do not consider how handsome or tall he is. I have not chosen him. I do not look at the things people look at. Man looks at how someone appears on the outside. But I look at what is in the heart."

1 SAMUEL 16:7 NIrV

A bodily disease which we look upon as whole and entire within itself, may, after all, be but a symptom of some ailment in the spiritual part.

NATHANIEL HAWTHORNE

To insure good health: Eat lightly, breathe deeply, live moderately, cultivate cheerfulness, and maintain an interest in life.

WILLIAM LONDEN

Common Sense

Good Thinking

The godly give good advice, but fools are destroyed by their lack of common sense.

PROVERBS 10:21 NLT

You've probably heard the expression "He doesn't have the sense he was born with." Have you ever thought about what that really means? It means that somewhere along the line, the person has lost the ability to exercise the sound judgment that God places in everyone before they are born. That innate sound judgment is also known as common sense—the ability to get along in life without the need for detailed instructions on each and every aspect of living.

God's way is the way of common sense. He created human beings to enjoy life and have fellowship with Him and with each other. He didn't create robots who need to be programmed; He instilled within each person the common sense he would need to take care of himself in order to enjoy both the life he was given and the fellowship of others—including his Creator. But along the way, many people lose some of the "good sense" they were born with as they become exposed to a multitude of ideas that run counter to God's intention for the way people should live.

What this means for you as a believer—especially as one who is venturing out into the world in a new and exciting way—is that you can trust the Bible as your commonsense guide through life. As you encounter new ideas and hear arguments for unbiblical theories, you can apply the "common sense" test. Take, for example, the idea that you can regularly hang out with people who are involved in a sin-drenched lifestyle without being negatively influenced by them. The Bible tells you to avoid those who live an ungodly life (Psalm 1:1–3, Proverbs 13:20, Proverbs 2:20); common sense should tell you the same thing. No matter how long, how hard, or how loud others may disagree with you, you know that spending an inordinate amount of time with sinful people will eventually affect you in the wrong way.

What are some other examples of biblical concepts that are rooted in common sense? For starters there's the foundational concept that you should live as the One who created you intended you to live. That just makes good sense, doesn't it? He intended you to live on good terms with Him, which means it makes sense to obey Him and worship Him and love Him as He loves you. He intended you to live on good terms with others, so all the biblical teachings about loving others and being kind and compassionate and practicing justice and honesty also make sense.

Common sense also applies in your very practical, day-to-day existence. Society tends to complicate the principles that can help you in your daily life, but many of them simply require sound judgment: Don't spend more money than you make. To lose weight, eat less and move more. Fill the tank before you run out of gas. Don't leave candles burning when you leave the house. Those are all examples of commonsense principles, and yet just about every day you hear of people who ignore those principles, sometimes with tragic consequences.

The good news is that you don't have to be among those who don't have the sense they were born with. Even if you've lost a measure of sound judgment along the way—and most people have—you can ask God to restore it to you, just as the psalmist did in Psalm 119:66. You can be sure that whatever God tells you through prayer or through your Bible reading, it will never run counter to the common sense He gave you when He created you.

All around you is the evidence of a world in which common sense is sorely lacking. Don't fall victim to the teachings of the world when your heart tells you that those teachings do not line up with the sound judgment God has given you. Trust the commonsense instincts God has placed within you and trust the good sense He has given to those whose counsel you respect. As you will soon discover, your ability to adjust to your new and independent lifestyle will depend a great deal on the extent to which you exercise your common sense.

I Will

Use sound judgment in my everyday life.   _yes_   _no_

Believe that God can give me an extra measure of
common sense.   _yes_   _no_

Realize that biblical teachings are steeped in
common sense.   _yes_   _no_

Ignore the wisdom of the world when it runs counter
to biblical teachings.   _yes_   _no_

Seek counsel only from those who exercise good
judgment.   _yes_   _no_

Be thankful for the good sense I was born with.   _yes_   _no_

Things to Do

☐ *Read Proverbs 1–2 to see what the Bible says about good judgment.*

☐ *Find at least one news story that indicates a person's lack of common sense.*

☐ *Memorize one or more Scriptures in this section.*

☐ *Start a journal page of commonsense sayings; make it as funny or serious as you like.*

☐ *Ask God to help you exercise sound judgment in a current situation in your life.*

☐ *For two days note all the times your common sense figured in to a decision you made.*

Things to Remember

[The psalmist wrote,] Train me in good common sense; I'm thoroughly committed to living your way.

PSALM 119:66 THE MESSAGE

[The Lord is] a rich mine of Common Sense for those who live well, a personal bodyguard to the candid and sincere.

PROVERBS 2:7 THE MESSAGE

Tune your ears to the world of wisdom; set your heart on a life of understanding.
Proverbs 2:2 THE MESSAGE

[Wisdom cries out,] "How naive you are! Let me give you common sense. O foolish ones, let me give you understanding."

PROVERBS 8:5 NLT

Dear friend, guard Clear Thinking and Common Sense with your life; don't for a minute lose sight of them.

PROVERBS 3:21 THE MESSAGE

The loose tongue of the godless spreads destruction; the common sense of the godly preserves them.

PROVERBS 11:9 THE MESSAGE

The law code itself is God's good and common sense, each command sane and holy counsel.

ROMANS 7:12 THE MESSAGE

Say to wisdom, "You are my sister," and call understanding your kinsman.

PROVERBS 7:4 NIV

[Solomon wrote,] Listen, my sons, to a father's instruction; pay attention and gain understanding.

PROVERBS 4:1 NIV

[Wisdom cries out,] "I am Lady Wisdom, and I live next to Sanity; Knowledge and Discretion live just down the street. The Fear-of-GOD means hating Evil, whose ways I hate with a passion—pride and arrogance and crooked talk. Good counsel and common sense are my characteristics; I am both Insight and the Virtue to live it out."

PROVERBS 8:12–14 THE MESSAGE

There is nothing as uncommon as common sense.

FRANK LLOYD WRIGHT

Success is more a function of consistent common sense than it is of genius.

AN WANG

Prayer

Two-Way Conversation

Be anxious for nothing, but in everything by prayer and supplication, with thanksgiving, let your requests be made known to God.

PHILIPPIANS 4:6 NKJV

Have you ever had a phone conversation in which the only thing you managed to say was an occasional "Uh-huh" or "Really?" or "Right, but . . ."? Everyone has. Some conversations could better be described as monologues, with one person doing all the talking and the other doing all the listening. That's not the way prayer is supposed to be, although sometimes people seem to forget that God would like to get a word in every now and then.

When you learn to think of prayer as a two-way conversation, with each party doing some of the listening as well as some of the talking, it becomes much easier to get into the habit of praying. Looking at prayer as a conversation rather than a monologue takes so much pressure off you—you have a whole lot less to say, and you can simply take a break and allow God to minister to you during your prayer time. What's more, you can talk to God throughout the day, simply turning your thoughts toward Him and being sensitive to the ways He may be communicating with you—through other people, through circumstances, through your reading of the Bible, and through your own thoughts, among others.

Your structured times of prayer can be as diverse as you want them to be. On one day you might try a form of prayer known as ACTS—an acronym standing for four steps of prayer, *adoration, confession, thanksgiving,* and *supplication* (or asking for things from God). The next day you might prefer writing out your prayer to God. On the following day you could simply pray the Lord's Prayer, meditating on each phrase and applying it to your current situation. Numerous resources, such as books, Web sites, and your pastoral leaders, can help you discover fresh ways to pray.

No matter how you pray, remember that God longs to have you open up a conversation with Him. He wants to hear from you. He wants you to be honest with Him about your fears and your needs and your concerns. He wants the opportunity to respond to you, both during your prayer time and throughout your day.

Regular prayer strengthens your faith and maintains an open and intimate relationship with the Father. You've reached a point in your life where you are more responsible than ever for maintaining that relationship—and by establishing a habit of prayer now, you can keep the lines of communication open between God and you in the future.

I Will

Set aside time each day to talk with God. _yes_ _no_

Understand that prayer is a two-way conversation. _yes_ _no_

Make prayer a vital part of my life by silently communicating with God throughout the day. _yes_ _no_

Learn to be open, honest, and vulnerable with God whenever I talk to Him. _yes_ _no_

Realize how much God longs to hear from me. _yes_ _no_

Be open to what God wants to say to me through prayer. _yes_ _no_

Keep my prayer life fresh by discovering new ways to pray. _yes_ _no_

Things to Do

☐ *Pray. Ask God to give you a heart for prayer.*

☐ *Discover different ways to pray; http://www.prayercentral.net/ is one of many excellent resources on prayer.*

☐ *Start a prayer journal in which you list the things you prayed about and how God answered your prayers.*

☐ *Join a prayer group or find a prayer partner.*

☐ *Give up one routine activity this week—such as watching a certain TV show—and replace that activity with a time of prayer.*

☐ *Learn to pray the Scriptures, using a resource such as http://www.prayitsayit.net/ or http://www.prayingscriptures.com/.*

Things to Remember

[John wrote,] This is the confidence we have in approaching God: that if we ask anything according to his will, he hears us.

1 JOHN 5:14 NIV

[Jesus said,] "Again I say to you that if two of you agree on earth concerning anything that they ask, it will be done for them by My Father in heaven. For where two or three are gathered together in My name, I am there in the midst of them."

MATTHEW 18:19–20 NKJV

Beloved, building yourselves up on your most holy faith; praying in the Holy Spirit; keep yourselves in the love of God, waiting anxiously for the mercy of our Lord Jesus Christ to eternal life.

JUDE 20–21 NASB

[Jesus said,] "Have faith that you will receive whatever you ask for in prayer."

MATTHEW 21:22 GOD'S WORD

[David wrote,] Listen to my voice in the morning, LORD. Each morning I bring my requests to you and wait expectantly.

PSALM 5:3 NLT

In prayer it is better to have a heart without words than words without a heart.

JOHN BUNYAN

Do not pray for easy lives. Pray to be stronger men. Do not pray for tasks equal to your powers. Pray for powers equal to your tasks.

PHILLIPS BROOKS

Procrastination

Delayed Reaction

Do not withhold good from those to whom it is due, when it is in the power of your hand to do so. Do not say to your neighbor, "Go, and come back, and tomorrow I will give it," when you have it with you.

PROVERBS 3:27–28 NKJV

"Catch up with you later." How many times have you said that—or have had it said to you? Fortunately, most of the time you do manage to "catch up" with others, but sometimes the temptation to let things slide can be pretty strong. That's especially true when it comes to maintaining relationships; it's easy to procrastinate when it comes to making that call or writing that letter or sending that email.

You may not automatically think of your relationships when you hear the word *procrastinate*. Most often, you've probably been told not to procrastinate in getting your schoolwork or your chores done. But relationships, whether they are with friends, family, or God, can also be affected by a person's tendency to procrastinate. On the flip side you honor others when you avoid putting them off until some unspecific "later" time. Now that you're becoming more independent, you won't always have someone else—like your parents—around to remind you to do that.

Did your mother call and leave a voice message asking you to phone home? Has your grandfather been expecting you to drop by for several weeks now? Have you followed up at all with that girl you prayed with last month? Have you made good on your pledge to spend quality time with the Lord each day—or are you putting that off until your schedule clears up? All these are examples of ways in which you could be procrastinating without even being fully aware of it.

Proverbs 3:27 admonishes you to not withhold good from those to whom it is due. That "good" can include tangible things like food or clothing, but it can also include intangible things, like a word of encouragement or a much-needed visit or a few minutes of your time, which simply show that you care. The Holy Spirit never seems to procrastinate when someone needs the "good" you can provide; He'll always let you know when someone has a need you can meet, but it's up to you to act on that knowledge in a timely way.

Overcoming the tendency to procrastinate is yet another aspect of growing toward maturity. Get in the habit of returning calls promptly and spending time with God early in the day—and catching up with others sooner rather than later. You'll quickly set yourself apart from the pack of procrastinators trailing behind you.

I Will

Be aware of how I tend to procrastinate when it comes to maintaining my relationships.

yes _no_

Commit myself to giving "good" to others when the Holy Spirit prompts me to.

yes _no_

Accept responsibility for remembering to fulfill my commitments to others in a timely manner.

yes _no_

Recognize the link between overcoming procrastination and becoming more mature.

yes _no_

Realize that I show honor to others by "catching up" with them sooner rather than later.

yes _no_

Show people I care about them by responding quickly to their needs.

yes _no_

Things to Do

☐ _Memorize Proverbs 3:27–28 or another verse in this section._

☐ _Ask God to show you those areas in your life in which you tend to procrastinate._

☐ _Contact at least one person who has been waiting to hear from you or expecting a visit from you._

☐ _Start a to-do list specifically for returning phone calls and other kinds of communication requiring a response from you._

☐ _Make a list of friends you've witnessed to and begin following up with them._

☐ _Set aside time early in the day to be with God; the sooner you meet with Him, the less likely you'll be to procrastinate._

Things to Remember

When you make a vow to God, do not delay fulfilling it; for he has no pleasure in fools. Fulfill what you vow.

ECCLESIASTES 5:4 NRSV

Since we are surrounded by so great a cloud of witnesses, let us lay aside every weight, and the sin which so easily ensnares us, and let us run with endurance the race that is set before us.

HEBREWS 12:1 NKJV

We desire that each one of you show the same diligence to the full assurance of hope until the end, that you do not become sluggish, but imitate those who through faith and patience inherit the promises.

HEBREWS 6:11–12 NKJV

He who has a slack hand becomes poor, but the hand of the diligent makes rich.

PROVERBS 10:4 NKJV

[The psalmist wrote,] I will hurry, without lingering, to obey your commands.

PSALM 119:60 NLT

Procrastination is the bad habit of putting of until the day after tomorrow what should have been done the day before yesterday.

NAPOLEON HILL

The wise does at once what the fool does at last.

BALTASAR GRACIAN

Diligence

Steady Output

The soul of a lazy man desires, and has nothing; but the soul of the diligent shall be made rich.

PROVERBS 13:4 NKJV

Do you know what often sets one worker apart from the others? It's the quality of diligence—the careful and intense attention to the task at hand. It's a quality that can even separate one hardworking employee from another hardworking employee; a diligent employee not only works hard but also remains alert to problems and perseveres when faced with challenges.

No matter what the future holds for you, you would be wise to cultivate the quality of diligence. You'll need it if you wish to excel in college or in military service or in a job—and you'll especially need it if your next stop is the mission field. Later on, parenthood will take every ounce of diligence you can muster. Master it now, and you'll find that your ability to apply concentrated effort to whatever you do will serve you well in the years to come.

God wants His people to be diligent. Not surprisingly,

the Bible has a great deal to say about diligence and its counterpart, laziness. The book of Proverbs is a great place to start if you want to find out what's in store for either the hard worker or the "sluggard"—the lazy, idle person. Here's a hint: You don't want to be caught acting the part of a sluggard. A life of idleness—whether it be the lifestyle of the rich and famous or that of a beach bum—may appear attractive, but it's an unsatisfying and ungodly way to live. God made you to be productive, to have your life count for something, to give your seventy or so years on earth a meaning beyond mere existence.

Make it a point to be diligent in every area of your life—your primary area of responsibility, such as a job or classwork if you're continuing on; your relationship with God and your spiritual growth; your responsibilities to your family and friends; and caring for your own physical, emotional, and spiritual needs. Does being diligent mean you have to work hard and be serious all the time? Certainly not. When the task at hand is fun, give careful and intense attention to having a great time. Your friends may just set you apart as one who really knows how to have fun—when it's time to have fun. Your keen sensitivity to God will let you know when that is.

I Will

Understand the benefit of applying diligence to what I do.   _yes_   _no_

Focus on the task at hand.   _yes_   _no_

Realize that God made me to be a productive person.   _yes_   _no_

Make my life on earth count for eternity.   _yes_   _no_

Be an attentive worker.   _yes_   _no_

Apply diligent effort to my spiritual life as well as my work.   _yes_   _no_

Recognize idleness as an unsatisfying way to live.   _yes_   _no_

Things to Do

☐ _List ways you can apply concentrated effort to your spiritual life._

☐ _Look up diligence on an online Bible search and read the corresponding verses._

☐ _Ask God to make you more diligent._

☐ _Copy one of the verses from Proverbs in this section and post it where you will see it often._

☐ _Come up with five recent situations in which you exhibited diligence._

☐ _Think of someone you would describe as a diligent person and list the ways he or she shows diligence._

Things to Remember

The hand of the diligent will rule, but the lazy man will be put to forced labor.

PROVERBS 12:24 NKJV

The plans of the diligent lead surely to plenty, but those of everyone who is hasty, surely to poverty.

PROVERBS 21:5 NKJV

The man Jeroboam was a mighty man of valor; and Solomon, seeing that the young man was industrious, made him the officer over all the labor force of the house of Joseph.

1 KINGS 11:28 NKJV

[A virtuous wife] is a hard worker, strong and industrious. She knows the value of everything she makes, and works late into the night.

PROVERBS 31:17-18 GNT

No matter how much a lazy person may want something, he will never get it. A hard worker will get everything he wants.

PROVERBS 13:4 GNT

He who labors diligently need never despair; for all things are accomplished by diligence and labor.

MENANDER OF ATHENS

Follow the tasks of your calling carefully and diligently.

RICHARD BAXTER

Spiritual Life

Just Like Breathing

On the last day, that great day of the feast, Jesus stood and cried out, saying, "If anyone thirsts, let him come to Me and drink. He who believes in Me, as the Scripture has said, out of his heart will flow rivers of living water."

JOHN 7:37–38 NKJV

You've come a long way in two decades, from a physically helpless newborn to a maturing young adult. Spiritually, however, you should continue to grow throughout the remainder of your life. But unlike physical growth, which happens naturally, spiritual growth results from intentional spiritual activity. The more attention you give to your spiritual life—the more you are able to integrate spirituality into your everyday existence—the more likely it is that your spiritual growth will come as naturally to you as breathing does right now.

Spirituality begins with a deep hunger and thirst for the things of God. That may sound like just so much religious talk, but the Bible frequently equates your need for God with your need for food and water. When you are really hungry, will anything but food stop the growling in your stomach in a satisfying way? When you are really thirsty, will anything but the right kind of liquid, such as water, quench that thirst? In the same way, when you need spiritual nourishment and hydration, only God will satisfy your spirit. That's no accident; He designed you to need Him, because He loves you and knows what is best for you. He alone can meet your deepest needs.

People who are continually growing spiritually are those who have learned to see the things that happen to them from a spiritual perspective, because they understand God's continual activity in their lives. That doesn't mean that you have to stop and analyze every little thing; it does mean that there will be times when the Spirit of God will prompt you to pay special attention to an event in your life, and that's when you need to stop and ask God what He wants you to see.

Often, He will get your attention through major events, such as a personal crisis or loss, or through puzzling events, like a closed door that you were certain was open to you. But He can just as readily try to get your attention through a routine activity, like a conversation with a coworker. Being alert to His prompting helps you to identify those times when He wants you to focus on a problem or encounter from a spiritual perspective. All that means is that you need to stop and ask Him, What are You trying to show me through this situation?

You can become more sensitive to what God is saying and doing in your life by spending more time with Him, praying, listening, reading His word, worshiping Him privately and communally, and obeying what you already know He wants you to do. Each God-related activity you immerse yourself in builds on the foundation you've already established. For example, when you first started reading the Gospels, you probably zeroed in on Jesus' parable and the narrative accounts of all that He did. Now, though, you gain new insights into biblical truth each time you read those same parables. That's an indication of spiritual growth, and it's part of what nurtures your spiritual sensitivity. In a similar way, when you first came to faith in Christ, you may have felt somewhat self-conscious when you prayed, but now that you've been praying for a while, you find it easier to come into the presence of God without thinking about yourself.

The coming years will be a busy time for you, as you take on additional responsibilities and try to sort out the new and varied challenges you encounter on a regular basis. Believers who neglect their spiritual life as they try to navigate their way into adulthood have a much tougher time of it. You can give yourself a much-needed edge by relying on God more than ever as you go about both the ordinary and extraordinary activities of your daily life. In time your dependence on the Lord will become like a second nature to you. Just as you don't consciously think about your physical growth as it is happening, there will be times when you will respond to a situation from a spiritual perspective without even being aware that that's what you did. Your spiritual response will come naturally—just like breathing.

I Will

Realize the importance of maintaining my
spiritual life.   yes   no

Understand what it means to hunger and thirst
after God.   yes   no

Learn to look at life from a spiritual perspective.   yes   no

Expect to glean new insights whenever I read
the Bible.   yes   no

Be sensitive to the Spirit of God in my daily activities.   yes   no

Realize that spiritual maturity takes time.   yes   no

Rely on God to teach me through my experiences.   yes   no

Things to Do

☐ *Ask several Christians you admire how they maintain their spiritual life.*

☐ *List the God-related activities you can do each day to grow spiritually.*

☐ *Ask God to reveal a new insight from your Bible reading today.*

☐ *Memorize one of the verses from Psalms listed in this section.*

☐ *Write in your journal about how the Thomas Merton quotation applies to you.*

☐ *List your spiritual goals (such as becoming more comfortable praying in public or sharing the gospel).*

☐ *Ask the Lord to help you understand a situation in your life from a spiritual perspective.*

Things to Remember

[David wrote,] Oh God, you are my God; at dawn I search for you. My soul thirsts for you. My body longs for you in a dry, parched land where there is no water.

PSALM 63:1 GOD'S WORD

[Jesus said,] "'You shall love the LORD your God with all your heart, with all your soul, with all your mind, and with all your strength.' This is the first commandment."

MARK 12:30 NKJV

[The psalmist wrote,] As the deer pants for the water brooks, so pants my soul for You, O God.
Psalm 42:1 NKJV

[David wrote,] He restores my soul; He leads me in the paths of righteousness for His name's sake.

PSALM 23:3 NKJV

[Jesus said,] "The thief does not come except to steal, and to kill, and to destroy. I have come that they may have life, and that they may have it more abundantly."

JOHN 10:10 NKJV

Oh, taste and see that the LORD is good;
blessed is the man who trusts in Him!

PSALM 34:8 NKJV

Jesus answered [the devil], saying, "It is
written, 'Man shall not live by bread
alone, but by every word of God.'"

LUKE 4:4 NKJV

Blessed be the God and Father of our
Lord Jesus Christ, who has blessed us
with every spiritual blessing in the
heavenly places in Christ.

EPHESIANS 1:3 NKJV

You also, as living stones, are being built
up a spiritual house, a holy priesthood,
to offer up spiritual sacrifices acceptable
to God through Jesus Christ.

1 PETER 2:5 NKJV

[Paul wrote,] Now we have received, not
the spirit of the world, but the Spirit
who is from God, that we might know
the things that have been freely given to
us by God. These things we also speak,
not in words which man's wisdom
teaches but which the Holy Spirit
teaches, comparing spiritual things
with spiritual.

1 CORINTHIANS 2:12–13 NKJV

**Christian
spirituality does
not begin with us
talking about our
experience; it
begins with
listening to God
call us, heal us,
forgive us.**

EUGENE S. PETERSON

**It is in the ordinary
duties and labors
of life that the
Christian can and
should develop his
spiritual union
with God.**

THOMAS MERTON

Regrets

Past Imperfect

Godly sorrow produces repentance leading to salvation, not to be regretted; but the sorrow of the world produces death.

2 CORINTHIANS 7:10 NKJV

Now that you are ready to take on a whole new set of challenges in your life, you may be looking back on the recent years of your life with a certain amount of regret. After all, you have a lot of questions about your future. Would college have been easier if you had applied yourself a bit more in high school? How about your spiritual life— do you wish you had paid a bit more attention to the biblical principles that would help you resist temptation?

Those are all questions that are rooted in regret, and thankfully, they're all questions that can be answered by going to God and asking Him to transform your regrets into a power for good in your future. You can count on Him to help you meet the academic challenges you face and to help you resist temptation—and whatever it is that concerns you about your future.

What about your past? Maybe you came to faith in

Christ after you had spent many of your teenage years living in a way that you now realize was contrary to the way He wanted you to live. Or perhaps you came to faith years ago but fell away and gave in to temptation during the time you were away from God. You now regret some of the things you did, things that can never be changed or reversed. Is there any hope that you can live with the terrible sense of regret that sometimes comes over you? Yes—there is hope, and that hope is very real.

Many people who have experienced deep regret have likewise experienced the incomparable depth of God's love. The God who brought you to a life of faith is the same God who will bring you to a life of joy and freedom—and that includes freedom from the pain of the past. As you bring your regrets to God, He can transform each one into a power for good in your future. You cannot change your past, but you can change your future by placing it in the hands of the One who loves you more than you can ever know. He's the One who wants you to keep your eyes on Him and on the promises He's made to you—promises that will enable you to live an abundant, regret-free life now and in the years to come.

I Will

Learn from my past mistakes.   *yes*   *no*

Realize the consequences of all my actions.   *yes*   *no*

Be excited about the future.   *yes*   *no*

Remember that God forgave and forgot my sins.   *yes*   *no*

Trust God to help me make better choices in the future.   *yes*   *no*

Realize that looking back often brings unnecessary pain.   *yes*   *no*

Know that I can have hope.   *yes*   *no*

Things to Do

☐ *Throw away any items that remind you of a past regret.*

☐ *List your regrets, pray about them, and throw the list away.*

☐ *Ask God to give you a picture of your regret-free future.*

☐ *Help a friend experience God's forgiveness for past mistakes.*

☐ *Memorize Psalm 103:12.*

☐ *Ask a trusted adult how he or she dealt with regrets.*

☐ *Resolve to obey God and avoid regret in the future.*

Things to Remember

How far has the LORD taken our sins from us? Farther than the distance from east to west!

PSALM 103:12 CEV

Repent therefore and be converted, that your sins may be blotted out, so that times of refreshing may come from the presence of the Lord.

ACTS 3:19 NKJV

[The one who recognizes the goodness of God] will not dwell unduly on the days of his life, because God keeps him busy with the joy of his heart.

ECCLESIASTES 5:20 NKJV

[The Lord] has made everything beautiful in its time. Also He has put eternity in [people's] hearts, except that no one can find out the work that God does from beginning to end.

ECCLESIASTES 3:11 NKJV

The weapons of our warfare are not carnal but mighty in God for pulling down strongholds, casting down arguments and every high thing that exalts itself against the knowledge of God, bringing every thought into captivity to the obedience of Christ.

2 CORINTHIANS 10:4-5 NKJV

Regret for time wasted can become a power for good in the time that remains, if we will only stop the waste and the idle, useless regretting.

ARTHUR BRISBANE

In history as in human life, regret does not bring back a lost moment and a thousand years will not recover something lost in a single hour.

STEFAN ZWEIG

Rest

Time-Out

[David wrote,] I will both lie down in peace, and sleep; for You alone, O Lord, make me dwell in safety.

PSALM 4:8 NKJV

For most students school is about as far from a leisurely, restful activity is you can get. On top of the school day, there are homework and sports and work and chores and church commitments—oh, and don't forget fun. Now that you've graduated, you may feel you've earned some well-deserved time off. In the back of your mind, though, you know that your life is about to get busy again, perhaps busier than ever. How will you cope with the new demands on your time, the demands that naturally come with gaining a greater degree of independence?

One of the best things you can do for yourself in the coming weeks and months is to get into the habit of taking time away from the routines of your life—a day of rest. God provided this for His people way back in the Old

Testament, but for many people the practice of taking a day of rest has fallen victim to the culture's 24/7 lifestyle. You can buck that trend by defying the culture and taking advantage of the day of rest God provided, one of the most underappreciated of all His gifts.

It would help, of course, if you had a clear idea of how you best relax. A day of rest for a friend might mean the craziness of an amusement park, but you'd really prefer a walk in the woods. If you need someone to help you get into the habit of slowing down for one day, then you know you need to find someone who will enjoy that walk in the woods as much as you do. No matter how you choose to unwind, make sure you place a high priority on taking that one day off. If a full day is impossible—if work or other mandatory obligations interfere with your best intentions—at least try to take part of a day off each week.

Remember, God took a day off after His six days of creation. Did He need a day off? No. He just wanted to enjoy the result of His work. He wanted to set an example for His people. He knew they would need a day off, even if He didn't. Why not follow His example? Enjoy the result of your hard work during the week with a well-deserved day off. You'll be recharged and better able to face the week ahead when you do.

I Will

Get the right amount of sleep each night. ___ yes ___ no

Recognize the Sabbath as a gift from God. ___ yes ___ no

Be aware of times when I am emotionally, physically, and spiritually fatigued. ___ yes ___ no

See time off as a way of recharging my energy. ___ yes ___ no

Relax in my own way rather than the way others might want me to. ___ yes ___ no

Get into the habit of taking up to a day off each week. ___ yes ___ no

Appreciate whatever amount of rest I can get. ___ yes ___ no

Things to Do

☐ Calculate how much rest you get in a week and decide if it's enough.

☐ Write a description of your ideal way to relax; do this on your day off.

☐ Schedule a Sabbath day and mark it on your calendar.

☐ Ask a friend to join you and help you keep your Sabbath commitment.

☐ Use an online Bible search to look up verses about rest.

☐ Ask God to make your night's sleep restful and reenergizing.

☐ Read the account of creation in Genesis 1–2.

Things to Remember

[Jesus said.] "Take My yoke upon you and learn from Me, for I am gentle and lowly in heart, and you will find rest for your souls."

MATTHEW 11:29 NKJV

[The Lord said to the Israelites through Moses,] "You shall proclaim on the same day that it is a holy convocation to you. You shall do no customary work on it. It shall be a statute forever in all your dwellings throughout your generations."

LEVITICUS 23:21 NKJV

[The psalmist wrote,] Return to your rest, O my soul, for the LORD has dealt bountifully with you.

PSALM 116:7 NKJV

[The Lord said,] "For I have satiated the weary soul, and I have replenished every sorrowful soul." After this I awoke and looked around, and my sleep was sweet to me.

JEREMIAH 31:25–26 NKJV

It is vain for you to rise up early, to sit up late, to eat the bread of sorrows; for so He gives His beloved sleep.

PSALM 127:2 NKJV

Because God is the Ceaseless Worker, we can afford to stop, and to rest, and to commit to him the arrears in our work, as well as the work done. *We* do not "bear up the pillars of the world." God does that.

ERIC S. ABBOTT

Men have conceived a twofold use of sleep: that it is a refreshing of the body in this life; that it is a preparing of the soul for the next.

JOHN DONNE

Reconcilable Differences

Let us pursue the things which make for peace and the things by which one may edify another.

ROMANS 14:19 NKJV

Unless you're fabulously wealthy, you will probably be sharing your living quarters with others your age, at least for the first few years you are on your own. Whether those "others" are college roommates selected at random by the housing department, your best friend, a barracks full of strangers, or someone you've just met at your first job, you'll discover fairly soon that living with your peers is not as easy or as fun as you hoped it would be. With a bit of patience, and a significant application of godly wisdom, your experience with your roommates can be an enriching one for everyone involved.

One of the keys to a good relationship with a roommate is the same one that's vital in any relationship: open and honest communication. If your roommate is a believer, then you both have an advantage, because you speak the same language and can appeal to each other on the basis of a shared belief in biblical truth. Even if your roommate is someone who does not share your faith in Christ, you can still apply biblical principles to your own behavior. Take the fruit of the spirit, for example: If you're having difficulties with your roommate, check to make sure you're exhibiting the "fruitful" qualities of love, joy, peace, patience, kindness, goodness, faithfulness, gentleness, and self-control in your encounters with her.

Living in peace with others requires a great deal of give and take. Always try to be the peacemaker in the relationship and rely on God to give you creative solutions to the problems you face. If your roommate is a night person and you are a morning person, for example, pray and ask God to help you come up with a schedule you can both live with. Be flexible; you may need to find another place to read or listen to music in order to accommodate your roommate's needs. That doesn't mean that you always have to be the accommodating one, but no matter how hard it is, Jesus does expect you to go the extra mile.

Above all else, never allow resentment to build up. If you find that you are feeling resentful toward your roommate, go to God immediately and talk to Him about your feelings. Ask Him to change your heart and give you an extra measure of grace as well as a deep love for your roommate. Your changed attitude could make an eternal difference in another person's life.

I Will

Strive to be a peacemaker.   *yes*   *no*

Learn to be a better communicator.   *yes*   *no*

Understand the importance of flexibility when living
with others.   *yes*   *no*

Get rid of resentment immediately.   *yes*   *no*

Seek God's wisdom in disputes with others.   *yes*   *no*

Go the extra mile to maintain my relationships.   *yes*   *no*

Seek to change myself rather than others.   *yes*   *no*

Things to Do

☐ *Pray for those you live with.*

☐ *Ask God to give you creative ideas for settling a dispute.*

☐ *List the things you need to change about yourself.*

☐ *Ask God for the grace and ability to make those changes.*

☐ *Journal about the daily challenges of living with others.*

☐ *Share your insights with someone who is currently in a roommate dispute.*

☐ *Ask a friend how he or she learned to deal with a roommate.*

Things to Remember

[Paul wrote,] To the Jews I became as a Jew, that I might win Jews; to those who are under the law, as under the law, that I might win those who are under the law; to those who are without law, as without law (not being without law toward God, but under law toward Christ), that I might win those who are without law; to the weak I became as weak, that I might win the weak. I have become all things to all men, that I might by all means save some.

1 CORINTHIANS 9:20–22 NKJV

Do not be unequally yoked together with unbelievers. For what fellowship has righteousness with lawlessness? And what communion has light with darkness?

2 CORINTHIANS 6:14 NKJV

Faithful are the wounds of a friend, but the kisses of an enemy are deceitful.

PROVERBS 27:6 NKJV

Pursue peace with all people, and holiness, without which no one will see the Lord.

HEBREWS 12:14 NKJV

One way of getting along with people is the ability to give in. Strength of character means the ability to give in to others from motives of love, kindness, and humility, and to do so gracefully, when no sin is involved. It also means the ability to stand on principle, and not to give in, when sin is involved.

LAWRENCE G. LOVASIK

There would be no society if living together depended upon understanding each other.

ERIC HOFFER

Time Management

Day by Day

---

*To everything there is a season, a time for every purpose
under heaven.*

ECCLESIASTES 3:1 NKJV

Throughout your life you've been exposed to time
management principles, whether you realized it or not.
Now that you've graduated, it's going to become more
important than ever to put those principles into action.
Unless you're going into military service, it's unlikely that
anyone will be there to monitor how you use your time; in
that sense you will be very much on your own.

Although God exists outside of time, the concept of
time was important enough to Him to place you within it.
God gave each person the same amount of time in a given
day, though the length of time spent on Earth varies with
each individual. What you do with that time on Earth is
critical to your own life and to those whose lives you
touch; the way you spend the time God has given you
shows Him how you appreciate His gift.

God wants you to spend your time wisely, balancing
your responsibilities with your need for rest and
relaxation. Time management doesn't just make you more

productive, though that's one outcome. It also frees up your schedule so you can enjoy the life you have. Fortunately, lots of people, including your peers, are willing to share their best time management principles. Most of them have withstood the test of—well, time.

Effective time managers usually point to organization as the primary means to the wise use of time. It's the old "a place for everything and everything in its place" message—one that may sound a bit too meticulous to you. Just adapt the truth behind it to your circumstances; if you regularly misplace your keys, for instance, you would save a lot of time by establishing a place for your keys—and keeping them there until you go out again. The same goes for any item or items that you use regularly.

A second means is an accurate understanding of how long it takes to accomplish something. Maybe you can hustle from your home to your appointment in five minutes, but face it—most days you don't feel like hustling, so realistically it takes closer to fifteen minutes. Allow fifteen minutes, not five. Also, you'll want to allow for interruptions and surprises in your schedule; if you drive to work, expect to hit every red light on the way, and figure that this will be the day the 212-car train will block the road you have to use.

A third means is to write down everything you have to do each day and prioritize the items on the list. Be sure to use some kind of planner. You can use something as simple as a spiral-bound notebook—just make sure you set that notebook aside for use only as a planner. Use your common sense when it comes to prioritizing. If you have a short project and a long project due at the same time, get the short one out of the way first; simply knowing that you've accomplished one of the two projects can give you a much-needed boost.

Use dead time to your advantage. In most states anyone who has ever applied for a driver's license knows how much time you can spend waiting at the DMV. Anticipate those situations and bring something to work on while you're waiting—a book, bills, your grocery list. Thinking ahead can often mean the difference between lost time and productive time.

There are many more time management principles, like learning to say no when people ask you to do things you clearly do not have time to do, and doing the most difficult tasks during your own unique "prime time"—the time of day when you are at your best. Many Internet sites offer dozens of other tips; do a search using terms that apply specifically to your situation, such as "time management college student" or "time management career."

Your best source for help with managing your time, of course, is the One who created time. Ask Him for His wisdom in scheduling your days. When you're planning your day, make sure you schedule in time alone with God. Remember—when you're prioritizing your daily to-do list, give top priority to that particular block of time.

I Will

Make use of the time management principles I have already learned.

yes _____ no _____

Realize that how I use my time is important to God.

yes _____ no _____

Make it a goal to become more organized.

yes _____ no _____

Spend my time wisely.

yes _____ no _____

Seek God's wisdom in planning my days.

yes _____ no _____

Be aware of how long certain tasks actually take.

yes _____ no _____

Learn to schedule difficult tasks for the time of day I'm at my best.

yes _____ no _____

Things to Do

☐ *Obtain—and resolve to use—a daily planner that best suits you (online, electronic, or paper).*

☐ *Organize your living space with time efficiency in mind.*

☐ *List your daily routine and estimate the time it takes to accomplish each item. Then actually time each item.*

☐ *Ask God to help you create a schedule and prioritize the tasks on it.*

☐ *Keep a running to-do list.*

☐ *Keep a book to read or something else to do in your car or backpack for those times when you're kept waiting.*

☐ *Figure out what your unique "prime time" is.*

Things to Remember

[God] says: "In an acceptable time I have heard you, and in the day of salvation I have helped you." Behold, now is the accepted time; behold, now is the day of salvation.

2 CORINTHIANS 6:2 NKJV

See then that you walk circumspectly, not as fools but as wise, redeeming the time, because the days are evil.

EPHESIANS 5:15–16 NKJV

> *He who keeps his command will experience nothing harmful; and a wise man's heart discerns both time and judgment.*
> Ecclesiastes 8:5 NKJV

Then [Nehemiah] told them, "Go, eat rich foods, drink sweet drinks, and send portions to those who cannot provide for themselves. Today is a holy day for the Lord. Don't be sad, because the joy you have in the LORD is your strength."

NEHEMIAH 8:10 GOD'S WORD

Remember now your Creator in the days of your youth, before the difficult days come, and the years draw near when you say, "I have no pleasure in them."

ECCLESIASTES 12:1 NKJV

[Mordecai said to Esther,] "If you remain completely silent at this time, relief and deliverance will arise for the Jews from another place, but you and your father's house will perish. Yet who knows whether you have come to the kingdom for such a time as this?"

ESTHER 4:14 NKJV

A thousand years in Your sight are like yesterday when it is past, and like a watch in the night.

PSALM 90:4 NKJV

Walk in wisdom toward those who are outside, redeeming the time.

COLOSSIANS 4:5 NKJV

Paul, a bondservant of God and an apostle of Jesus Christ, according to the faith of God's elect and the acknowledgment of the truth which accords with godliness, in hope of eternal life which God, who cannot lie, promised before time began, but has in due time manifested His word through preaching, which was committed to me according to the commandment of God our Savior.

TITUS 1:1–3 NKJV

In God, time and eternity are one and the same thing.

HENRY SUSO

Yesterday is history. Tomorrow is a mystery. And today? Today is a gift. That's why we call it the present.

BABATUNDE OLATUNJI

Solitude

In Seclusion

[Jesus] said to them, "Come aside by yourselves to a deserted place and rest a while."

MARK 6:31 NKJV

If you're like most of your peers, solitude is probably something you haven't given a whole lot of thought to. Sure, there were times you retreated to your room or some other private spot just to get away from other people for a while. Everyone needs that kind of aloneness in life. But there's another kind of solitude: Instead of needing to get away from other people, you find that you need to get alone with God. That kind of solitude is not so much a getting away from someone as a going toward Someone.

Before you graduated you were probably living at home, where you thought it was hard to find time alone. But now you're faced with other challenges: maybe a roommate who has a ton of friends over every night or a military barracks with dozens of other soldiers. Time alone with God? Where? When?

The answer to "when" is easier than it may seem. People do make time for the things that they enjoy, things that are important to them. No matter how busy your day is, you can find time to be alone with God if that's a priority in your life. "Where" might be a greater challenge, but remember this: God wants time alone with you as well, and He'll be sure to direct you to a place of solitude if you ask Him to. Even in the middle of a large city, there are places where you can find peace and quiet, like a safe park, a free art museum, a library, or a botanical garden. No one needs to know the real reason you are there—just find a quiet corner where you can be alone with God and your own thoughts.

Even Jesus needed times of solitude. He frequently got away from the crowds that followed Him and spent time alone with the Father. As always, His is an excellent pattern to follow. When you eventually find a time and place of solitude, you don't have to say a word. God knows what is in your heart, and whether you are in a public or a private place, all you need to do is listen for that still small voice inside as God ministers to you. He's been waiting for this moment, for the noise and commotion in your life to stop so He could share this special time with you.

I Will

Recognize the need for solitude.   ___yes___   ___no___

Learn from Jesus' example.   ___yes___   ___no___

Expect God to meet me in my times of solitude.   ___yes___   ___no___

Believe that I can experience solitude even in a
crowd.   ___yes___   ___no___

Learn to hear God's still, small voice.   ___yes___   ___no___

Believe that God wants to spend time with me.   ___yes___   ___no___

Make time alone with God a priority in my life.   ___yes___   ___no___

Things to Do

☐ *Find a place where you can experience solitude.*

☐ *Take your journal with you and write what comes to mind in your time alone with God.*

☐ *Ask God to show you where He fits in to your schedule.*

☐ *Read a portion of the Bible that deals with solitude, such as Psalm 62.*

☐ *Read the quotation by Amma Syncletica and write in your journal about how it applies to you.*

☐ *Ask several Christians how they spend their time alone with God.*

☐ *Memorize one or two verses from this section.*

Things to Remember

It is good that one should hope and wait quietly for the salvation of the LORD.

LAMENTATIONS 3:26 NKJV

[David wrote,] My soul, wait silently for God alone, for my expectation is from Him.

PSALM 62:5 NKJV

A time to tear, and a time to sew; a time to keep silence, and a time to speak.

ECCLESIASTES 3:7 NRSV

[Paul wrote,] You also aspire to lead a quiet life, to mind your own business, and to work with your own hands, as we commanded you.

1 THESSALONIANS 4:11 NKJV

[David wrote,] Surely I have calmed and quieted my soul, like a weaned child with his mother; like a weaned child is my soul within me.

PSALM 131:2 NKJV

It is possible to be solitary in one's mind while living in a crowd, and it is possible for one who is a solitary to live in the crowd of his own thoughts.

AMMA SYNCLETICA

Solitude is to the mind what diet is to the body.

MARQUIS DE VAUVENARGUES

Success

Golden Opportunity

This Book of the Law shall not depart from your mouth, but you shall meditate in it day and night, that you may observe to do according to all that is written in it. For then you will make your way prosperous, and then you will have good success.

JOSHUA 1:8 NKJV

Think of the one thing you'd like to be a success at in life. Maybe you want to be a first baseman for the New York Yankees and the proud owner of a World Series ring or two. Or your dream might be to follow in the footsteps of someone like Bill Gates and use your nerdiness to create a multibillion-dollar corporation. You might even want to be an evangelistic success and lead countless people to the Lord, the way Billy Graham and Luis Palau have.

What would it take, though, to find success in the specific area of life that appeals to you? Skill, talent, intelligence, a degree from a prestigious university, the right contacts—the luck of the draw? Many factors figure in to any successful person's journey. While your journey is in a sense just getting started, even before you graduated many of those factors were operating in your life already.

The most important one, though, is one you may not have considered, and that's your relationship with God.

Does that mean your relationship with God automatically ensures your success in the world's eyes? One look around the sanctuary on any given Sunday morning should convince you otherwise. You may see a few people who are considered a success by the community in which you live, but how many people in that community think of the word *success* when they look at the youth leader or the church secretary or the nursery workers? Yet in God's eyes those people are the success stories in His kingdom, the people who responded to Him in obedient service.

As a believer your chances of success in your chosen field are by all means better because of your relationship with God, as long as you seek His will and follow it and maintain a high degree of personal and professional integrity in your work. Just remember that God's definition of success does not always line up with that of the world's definition. Things that are important in the world's eyes—prestige, power, and wealth—are insignificant in God's eyes. He knows that the true measures of success are those things that seldom result in celebrity status, things like a heart turned fully toward Him and a deep sense of concern and compassion for the physical and spiritual well-being of others. The degree to which you serve God and others is the degree to which you will find true success in life.

I Will

Understand how God's view of success differs from the world's.

yes _no_

Rely on God to make me a success in His eyes.

yes _no_

Obey God and serve others.

yes _no_

Seek God's will throughout my life.

yes _no_

Learn to gauge my success by God's standard.

yes _no_

Realize that success is a lifelong journey.

yes _no_

Believe that God will direct me on the path to success.

yes _no_

Things to Do

☐ _Ask an older Christian what it takes to be a success._

☐ _Read a book or article on success from a Christian perspective._

☐ _List what you think will make you successful in your chosen field._

☐ _Now pray over that list and ask God to refine it._

☐ _Post either of the quotations on the next page on your mirror._

☐ _Ask your parents or a friend how you've been spiritually successful so far._

☐ _Read verses on success using an online Bible search._

Things to Remember

Meditate on these things; give yourself entirely to them, that your progress may be evident to all.

1 TIMOTHY 4:15 NKJV

[A wise person's] delight is in the law of the LORD, and in His law he meditates day and night. He shall be like a tree planted by the rivers of water, that brings forth it fruit in its season, whose leaf also shall not wither; and whatever he does shall prosper.

PSALM 1:2–3 NKJV

If you obey the laws and teachings that the LORD gave Moses, you will be successful. Be strong and brave and don't get discouraged or be afraid of anything

1 CHRONICLES 22:13 CEV

Respect your father and mother, and you will live a long and successful life in the land I am giving you.

DEUTERONOMY 5:16 CEV

[Paul wrote,] It is not that we think we can do anything of lasting value by ourselves. Our only power and success come from God.

2 CORINTHIANS 3:5 NLT

Size is not a measure of success. Faithfulness is a measure of success. Biblical fidelity is a measure of success.

CHARLES COLSON

It is not your business to succeed, but to do right; when you have done so, the rest lies with God.

C. S. LEWIS

Life Happens

Do not think it strange concerning the fiery trial which is to try you, as though some strange thing happened to you; but rejoice to the extent that you partake of Christ's sufferings, that when His glory is revealed, you may also be glad with exceeding joy.

1 PETER 4:12–13 NKJV

Among the things that you were probably not told when you came to faith in Christ was the reality that you would continue to face significant trials throughout your lifetime. In all fairness those who shared the gospel with you couldn't cover everything. What's more, they knew that you would be able to face those ordeals far better after you came to the Lord and had spent time learning to trust Him in ever deeper ways. That's the assurance that you can have now—as you step out on your own and face sometimes serious difficulties without your family nearby, you can trust God to see you through.

You can count on facing at least two types of trials in the coming years: those that result simply from being alive and those that result from your identification with Jesus Christ. Everyone who has ever lived has gone through difficult times; some people, it seems, get an extra dose of difficulty in the form of extreme poverty or debilitating physical problems or the tragic loss of several loved ones at one time. God's grace is available to each person as he or she attempts to cope with the trials they face, but it is often only those who already have a relationship with Him who seem to recognize that grace and draw on it.

The trials that result from your life as a child of God are another matter. Obviously, not everyone experiences those trials—not even every Christian. But the Bible makes it clear that believers not only are supposed to expect a "fiery trial" but they are also encouraged to rejoice in those trials. Peter so closely identified with Christ that he considered the ordeals of believers to be an unmatched opportunity to share in the suffering Christ endured on the cross. That's not a bad thing to focus on when you face persecution or ridicule or rejection because of your own identification with Jesus.

Believers who have gotten to the other side of a crisis will likely be the first to tell you that God's promises are true—every one of them. Your faith may be tested during difficult times, but it will also be strengthened and purified as you continue to trust the Lord throughout those times. God is your refuge and strength, your help in trouble. You can count on Him to give you the grace to see you through.

I Will

Understand that trials are a part of life.   *yes* _____   *no* _____

Understand that I can also expect to experience
trials because of my faith.   *yes* _____   *no* _____

Go to God as soon as I face a difficulty.   *yes* _____   *no* _____

Believe that God's promise to always be with me
is true.   *yes* _____   *no* _____

Learn to rejoice and praise God in the midst
of trials.   *yes* _____   *no* _____

Recognize and draw on the grace God offers.   *yes* _____   *no* _____

Help others going through difficulties.   *yes* _____   *no* _____

Things to Do

☐ *Memorize 1 Peter 4:12–13.*

☐ *Ask God to prepare you for the trials you will certainly face in your life.*

☐ *Meditate on the first chapter of James.*

☐ *Read a good book on the persecution of Christians, such as dc Talk's Jesus Freaks.*

☐ *Pray for persecuted Christians around the world (visit sites like www.persecution.org and www.persecutedchurch.org for more information).*

☐ *Pray with someone who is going through a trial right now.*

☐ *Listen to Mark Schultz's song, "I Have Been There."*

Things to Remember

God is our refuge and strength, a very present help in trouble.

PSALM 46:1 NKJV

Consider it all joy, my brethren, when you encounter various trials.

JAMES 1:2 NASB

In this you greatly rejoice, though now for a little while, if need be, you have been grieved by various trials, that the genuineness of your faith, being much more precious than gold that perishes, though it is tested by fire, may be found to praise, honor, and glory at the revelation of Jesus Christ.

1 PETER 1:6–7 NKJV

If you faint in the day of adversity, your strength is small.

PROVERBS 24:10 NKJV

[Wisdom cries out,] "Whoever listens to me will dwell safely, and will be secure, without fear of evil."

PROVERBS 1:33 NKJV

No pressure, no diamonds.

MARY CASE

God wishes to test you like gold in the furnace. The dross is consumed by the fire, but the pure gold remains and its value increases.

JEROME EMILIANI

Motives

Wise Whys

All the ways of a man are clean in his own sight, but the LORD weighs the motives.

PROVERBS 16:2 NASB

Imagine if you can what would happen if this scene were played out at the next church service you attend: The sanctuary is quiet as a hush falls over the congregation. Something big is about to happen; you can feel it in the air. Suddenly, the choir stands and the organist sounds the first notes of "Hallelujah" from Handel's *Messiah*. The doors to the sanctuary open wide, admitting a local dignitary and his entourage. With a flourish the dignitary makes his way down the aisle to the altar.

At just the right moment, as if on cue, he reaches into his breast pocket, pulls out a check, and places it in the collection plate. Triumphantly he leaves the church just as he entered it, with a great deal of fanfare and a retinue of admirers. The congregation looks on in awe and appreciation. Applause bursts out with Handel's music ringing in the background. All that for a donation to the church? Who does he think he is? You and your friends put your check in every week, and nobody makes a fuss about it. What's the deal?

That scene is not likely to take place in reality, but that's pretty much the way Jesus depicted the hypocrites—the scribes and Pharisees—of His day. They gave to the poor all right, but they did it only to be seen by the masses and considered righteous by their peers. They no more wanted to help the poor than your local dignitary wanted to leave an anonymous gift. Their motivation in giving was public adulation, not genuine concern and compassion for others.

As you'll notice throughout Scripture, your motives are important to God. He sees your heart, and He knows if the things you do stem from pure motives—or self-serving motives. He wants His people to serve Him with their whole heart, not from a heart divided by selfish desires.

Over the next few years, you will have a whole new set of life experiences. In those experiences, you will be exposed to people who will operate from a dazzling array of motives. Some will do seemingly good things but for all the wrong reasons, like the misguided character on a popular sitcom who converted to another faith just to woo a particular woman and win her love. When it comes to proclaiming the gospel, ulterior motives date all the way back to the first century, when a rival Christian faction sprang up simply, it seems, to discredit the apostle Paul.

If you are faithful in following Christ, you are no doubt genuinely serving God with pure motives. But everyone is tempted at times to do "spiritual" things for selfish reasons. Sometimes it's because they want to impress others, or because there's a tangible payoff involved, like financial gain, or because they need to feel like a success. You may face those and other temptations some day, but when you do, you can be sure that the Holy Spirit will get your attention through a "check" in your spirit. That's a momentary hesitation, an awareness that all is not right with what you're about to do. People who ignore that check are those who fall into sin. Pay attention when the Holy Spirit places a check on your spirit; it always signals trouble ahead.

Pay close attention not only to what you do but also to why you do it. Are you serving God out of a genuine love for Him? Are you involved in a particular ministry because you believe in its mission? Do you cheerfully give to the church because you want to further the work of the kingdom of God? Do you find great joy in doing things for other people without them ever finding out who it was that blessed them? Is at least some of your work for God accomplished behind the scenes, away from the bright lights and public recognition? If so—if you can answer yes to those and similar questions—you can be confident that you are serving God with pure motives. God sees your heart, and He is well-pleased with the way you bring honor and glory to His name.

People may be pure in their own eyes,
but the LORD examines their motives.
—PROVERBS 16:2 NLT

I Will

Examine my motives.   *yes*   *no*

Understand that God sees my heart.   *yes*   *no*

Be sensitive to the Holy Spirit's "checks."   *yes*   *no*

Serve God in ways that no one else can see.   *yes*   *no*

Honor God by serving Him with pure motives.   *yes*   *no*

Understand that why I do something is as
important as what I do.   *yes*   *no*

Trust God to deliver me from the temptation to do
good things for wrong reasons.   *yes*   *no*

Things to Do

☐ *Read about the way the hypocrites gave money to the poor in Matthew 6:1–4.*

☐ *Listen to the Newsboys' CD Shine, which contains lots of songs about believers' motives.*

☐ *List as many reasons as you can think of for why a person would get involved in, say, a ministry to the poor. Determine which reasons stem from pure motives.*

☐ *Now list the reasons why you are involved in a particular ministry and decide if your motive for involvement is pure.*

☐ *Write in your journal about what your motives are for choosing the career path you've decided on.*

☐ *Ask God to make you more sensitive to the reasons you do certain things, especially in serving Him.*

Things to Remember

[Paul wrote,] To this end we both labor and suffer reproach, because we trust in the living God, who is the Savior of all men, especially of those who believe.

1 TIMOTHY 4:10 NKJV

Bondservants, be obedient to those who are your masters according to the flesh, with fear and trembling, in sincerity of heart, as to Christ.

EPHESIANS 6:5 NKJV

He who has a deceitful heart finds no good, and he who has a perverse tongue falls into evil.
Proverbs 17:20 NKJV

[David said,] "As for you, my son Solomon, know the God of your father, and serve Him with a loyal heart and with a willing mind; for the LORD searches all hearts and understands all the intent of the thoughts. If you seek Him, He will be found by you; but if you forsake Him, He will cast you off forever."

1 CHRONICLES 28:9 NKJV

Counsel in the heart of man is like deep water, but a man of understanding will draw it out.

PROVERBS 20:5 NKJV

You ask and do not receive, because you ask amiss, that you may spend it on your pleasures.

JAMES 4:3 NKJV

The spirit of a man is the lamp of the LORD, searching all the inner depths of his heart.

PROVERBS 20:27 NKJV

[Paul wrote,] We didn't have any hidden motives when we won you over, and we didn't try to fool or trick anyone. God was pleased to trust us with his message. We didn't speak to please people, but to please God who knows our motives.

1 THESSALONIANS 2:3–4 CEV

Hear in heaven Your dwelling place, and forgive, and act, and give to everyone according to all his ways, whose heart You know (for You alone know the hearts of all the sons of men).

1 KINGS 8:39 NKJV

[David wrote,] Search me, O God, and know my heart; try me and know my anxieties.

PSALM 139:23 NKJV

In the fulfillment of your duties, let your intentions be so pure that you reject from your actions any other motive than the glory of God and the salvation of souls.

ANGELA MERICI

The saint does everything that any other decent person does, only somewhat better and with a totally different motive.

COVENTRY PATMORE

Work

Just a Job?

Whatever you do, do it heartily, as to the Lord and not to men, knowing that from the Lord you will receive the reward of the inheritance; for you serve the Lord Christ.

COLOSSIANS 3:23–24 NKJV

No doubt about it, work is a fact of life. Few people can get through life without having a job of some sort, and for most graduates that "sort" is a low-paying, entry-level job. For a while, at least, you may be the one changing the toner in the copier or making the coffee every time the pot is empty. When there's dirty or menial or mind-numbing work to be done, you know who's most likely to be called on to do it—you.

The way you respond to the work you are asked to do—and to the one who asks you to do it—can make all the difference in the way your day goes. Maintain a cheerful attitude, and you'll have a better day; refuse to join in your coworkers' gripe sessions, and you'll find less to complain about; talk about your job in a positive way, and you might actually start to like it more. Those are some of the ways others have learned to cope with a job that's something less than their dream job. Try them for a week; you'll probably have a better week as a result.

As a believer you have an even better reason to respond favorably to the work you do: Your commitment to serve Jesus Christ in all that you do. That, of course, includes your job. An entry-level job in particular is an important training ground for the future. When you learn to see the Lord as your Boss in the early years of your career, then later on—perhaps when you yourself are the boss—you will understand that even in positions of higher responsibility, the Lord is still your Boss. Think of how much better every workplace would be if the earthly boss had that understanding.

Over the course of your life, you'll hold numerous jobs. But no matter how many human bosses you have, you will always have one Boss who accompanies you throughout your career. He's the one only one you can count on to always be there for you, to always have your best interests at heart, to always help you do the very best work you can possibly do. Remember to thank Him for all that He does for you throughout the workday. Most important of all, commit your work to Him; He'll never mind sharing the dirty work with you.

I Will

Maintain a positive attitude toward my work. _____ yes _____ no

Realize that an entry-level job is an important training ground. _____ yes _____ no

Work as if I am working for the Lord. _____ yes _____ no

Be thankful for whatever job I hold. _____ yes _____ no

Realize that work is a fact of life. _____ yes _____ no

Strive to be a good example to my coworkers. _____ yes _____ no

Commit my work to the Lord. _____ yes _____ no

Things to Do

☐ *Pray for your boss and coworkers.*

☐ *Ask God to show you ways in which you could be a better worker.*

☐ *Think of someone you consider to be a good worker and determine what it is that makes her so good at what she does.*

☐ *Memorize Colossians 3:23–24 and 2 Thessalonians 3:10.*

☐ *Personalize George Smith Patton's quotation for your situation.*

☐ *Come up with three positive statements you can make about your job.*

☐ *List some things you could do to be a better worker.*

Things to Remember

[Paul wrote,] Even when we were with you, we commanded you this: If anyone will not work, neither shall he eat.

2 THESSALONIANS 3:10 NKJV

People go out to do their work and keep working until evening.

PSALM 104:23 GNT

Remain in the same house, eating and drinking such things as they give, for the laborer is worthy of his wages. Do not go from house to house.

LUKE 10:7 NKJV

Whatever your hand finds to do, do it with your might; for there is no work or device or knowledge or wisdom in the grave where you are going.

ECCLESIASTES 9:10 NKJV

[God said to Adam,] "In the sweat of your face you shall eat bread till you return to the ground, for out of it you were taken; for dust you are, and to dust you shall return."

GENESIS 3:19 NKJV

Work will win when wishy washy wishing won't.

THOMAS S. MONSON

If a man is called a street-sweeper, he should sweep streets even as Michelangelo painted, or Beethoven composed music, or Shakespeare wrote poetry. He should sweep streets so well that all the hosts of heaven and earth will pause to say, Here lived a great street-sweeper who did his job well.

GEORGE SMITH PATTON

Worship

Fit for a King

Give unto the LORD the glory due to His name; worship the LORD in the beauty of holiness.

PSALM 29:2 NKJV

When many people hear the word *worship*, they are likely to think of a church setting. Maybe they are reminded of a sacred concert, or they believe the word applies to the hymn-singing and prayer at church on Sunday morning, or they simply equate worship with attending a worship service. But one of the best aspects of worship is its true purpose—giving reverent honor and adoration to God. That is something you can do anywhere.

As you gradually experience ever-greater degrees of self-sufficiency, you may discover that your experience of worshiping God will begin to mature. Living at home and leading a busy life that revolved around school, you may have enjoyed true times of worshiping God only at church or youth group meetings. Those times of communal worship are still important, and especially if you are leaving home, you'll want to find a church or a small group of believers—or both—with whom you can continue to express your deep love and awe of God.

Even so, you can also use this time of newfound independence to begin to cultivate private times of worship. Any time your thoughts turn toward God can become a worship experience, no matter where you are. It's easier, of course, when you are alone; then you can give voice to your adoration of God through prayer and singing and even reading worshipful Scripture passages aloud. But even in a crowded subway or in noisy traffic you can experience true worship as your spirit gives reverence to God. The more often you worship Him in the presence of others, the easier it gets.

If you're going through a rough time—particularly if God seems far away or uninvolved in your life—you may be tempted to forget all about worshiping God. You may experience a similar temptation when you are distracted by the busyness of your day-to-day existence. Those are the times when it's especially important to continue worshiping the One who created you. Make sure you have access to a good selection of praise and worship music for those times when you need something extra to help you get into a worshipful frame of mind and spirit. As you focus on God and all that He is, the things you considered urgent just minutes before are likely to appear to be much less important—and God Himself is likely to appear to be that much closer to you.

I Will

Learn to worship God in private.   *yes*   *no*

Understand the importance of continuing in
communal worship.   *yes*   *no*

Realize that I can worship God anywhere, at
any time.   *yes*   *no*

Continue to worship God even when He seems
far away.   *yes*   *no*

Recognize the different ways of worshiping God.   *yes*   *no*

Use worship music or Scripture passages to help me
get in the right frame of mind.   *yes*   *no*

Things to Do

- [ ] *Listen to a good worship CD, such as Michael W. Smith's* Worship *or* Worship Again.

- [ ] *Talk to a worship leader about how he tries to bring people into the presence of God.*

- [ ] *List the various ways you can worship God and use each one at different times.*

- [ ] *Spend time in prayer simply giving honor and adoration to God.*

- [ ] *Get together with some friends for a time dedicated to worshiping God.*

- [ ] *Do a Bible search for words like worship, adoration, and reverence.*

Things to Remember

[Jesus said,] "The hour is coming, and now is, when the true worshipers will worship the Father in spirit and truth; for the Father is seeking such to worship Him. God is Spirit, and those who worship Him must worship in spirit and truth."

JOHN 4:23–24 NKJV

The LORD will be awesome to them, for He will reduce to nothing all the gods of the earth; people shall worship Him, each one from his place, indeed all the shores of the nations.

ZEPHANIAH 2:11 NKJV

[David wrote,] I will worship toward Your holy temple, and praise Your name for Your lovingkindness and Your truth; for You have magnified Your word above all Your name.

PSALM 138:2 NKJV

Oh, worship the LORD in the beauty of holiness! Tremble before Him, all the earth.

PSALM 96:9 NKJV

All the ends of the world shall remember and turn to the LORD, and all the families of the nations shall worship before You.

PSALM 22:27 NKJV

We should dedicate ourselves to becoming in this life the most perfect worshipers of God we can possibly be, as we hope to be through all eternity.

BROTHER ANDREW

God is not moved or impressed with our worship until our hearts are moved and impressed by him.

KELLY SPARKS

Zeal

Full Speed Ahead

[David wrote,] Passion for your house burns within me, so those who insult you are also insulting me.

PSALM 69:9 NLT

Think of the last time you saw the word *zealous* in print—anywhere but in a Christian publication. It probably carried a negative connotation. Politicians are often described as zealous in their relentless pursuit of an unpopular cause; the word is also applied to police officers charged with brutality. But a zealous person, in the actual definition of the word, is simply one who is passionate and enthusiastic about a person or a cause. A zealous Christian, then, is one who is passionate and enthusiastic about Christ and His kingdom.

Why the negative connotation? Because some people overdo it by expecting others to have the same level of passion that they have. How then can you share your passion for Christ without overdoing it, as your postgraduation circle of friends and acquaintances widens to include many who do not know the Lord? The answer lies in your commitment to becoming more like Christ Himself.

Look at the way He served the Father and lived His life; His zeal for the things of God were unmatched, but so was His compassion for the people who so desperately needed God. His zealous, righteous anger was reserved for those who knowingly abused their spiritual power and the house of God, the Pharisees and the moneychangers. When it came to those who had been led astray—the sheep without a shepherd—Jesus' zeal took the form of tenderness and kindness.

Make it your primary goal in life to become more like Christ. No one else—not the disciples who sat at His feet or the apostles who first spread the gospel or any other believer who has ever lived—is worthy of imitation. When you follow His pattern for living, you can remain passionate for the things of God without fear of overdoing it. Will some people reject you? Of course. After all, they rejected Him. But if your zeal for the Lord is characterized by kindness and compassion in your dealings with others, you can have the assurance that you have been a good witness for the God you serve.

Don't allow the added responsibilities in your life to distract you from the things of God. Instead, let your zeal for the things of God steer the course of your life. Your passion and enthusiasm for Christ and His kingdom could have a lasting effect on the countless people whose lives will intersect with yours in the coming years.

I Will

Be zealous for God without expecting others to share my level of passion.

yes _no_

Treat believers and unbelievers alike with compassion.

yes _no_

Make it a goal to become more Christlike.

yes _no_

Strive to be a good witness for God.

yes _no_

Keep my focus on the things of God despite my busyness.

yes _no_

Believe that God will help me balance my enthusiasm for Him with a concern for others.

yes _no_

Things to Do

☐ _Read the Gospel of Mark, noting the way Jesus responded to different individuals and groups of people._

☐ _List the qualities that you believe qualify as Christlike. Determine which you need to work on first._

☐ _Recall a time when someone you knew was overzealous and think of how he came across to unbelievers._

☐ _Pray for those who may have rejected Christ as a result of your friend's witness._

☐ _Now think of a time when someone's passion for Christ was a good witness, and determine what you could learn from that experience._

☐ _Memorize at least one of the Scriptures or quotations about zeal._

Things to Remember

[Paul wrote,] Brethren, my heart's desire and prayer to God for Israel is that they may be saved. For I bear them witness that they have a zeal for God, but not according to knowledge.

ROMANS 10:1–2 NKJV

The LORD shall go forth like a mighty man; He shall stir up His zeal like a man of war. He shall cry out, yes, shout aloud; He shall prevail against His enemies.

ISAIAH 42:13 NKJV

[The psalmist wrote,] My zeal has consumed me, because my enemies have forgotten Your words.

PSALM 119:139 NKJV

Observe this very thing, that you sorrowed in a godly manner: What diligence it produced in you, what clearing of yourselves, what indignation, what fear, what vehement desire, what zeal, what vindication! In all things you proved yourselves to be clear in this matter.

2 CORINTHIANS 7:11 NKJV

If thou shalt remain faithful and zealous in labor, doubt not that God shall be faithful and bountiful in rewarding thee.

THOMAS À KEMPIS

If once our hearts were but filled with zeal for God, and compassion for people's souls, we would up and be doing, though we could but lay a brick a day, and God would be with us.

WILLIAM GURNALL

Transitions

Changing Times

[The Lord said,] "Behold, I will do a new thing, now it shall spring forth; shall you not know it? I will even make a road in the wilderness and rivers in the desert."

ISAIAH 43:19 NKJV

There's no question about it: You are undergoing one of the biggest transitions of your life. You heard it in all the graduation speeches; you read it in all the greeting cards and e-mails congratulating you as you enter this new phase of your life; you saw it on the faces of your relatives—especially your parents. This is a very, very big deal. There's no turning back from it.

Despite your uncertainty about what the future holds for you, this can be one of the most exciting times of transition in your life, a time you'll look back on with a sense of satisfaction and pleasure. Yes, you are facing many changes, some of which may seem a bit intimidating—or even frightening—from where you stand right now. But as long as where you stand is in the center of God's will, you have no need to cower in fear. You can face your future and all the coming changes with enthusiasm and optimism.

Those changes, of course, are inevitable. Everything changes; God is the only thing in the whole universe that will never change. He will always be steadfast and true to you and to His Word, and He wants to make sure you know that you have nothing to worry about as you leave so much of the familiar behind. He is doing a new thing in your life, and that new thing is a good thing. He will be with you every step of the way.

Are you about to change your address? He'll make the move with you. Will you be leaving your old friends behind? He'll be your closest friend even as you strive to make new friends. Are you launching out on your own financially? He'll provide for your needs as you learn how to live from paycheck to paycheck. Will you be on unfamiliar turf when it comes to the type of church you'll be attending? He'll guide you through your initial discomfort and open your eyes to new ways of worshiping Him.

The bottom line is this: No matter what your circumstance, God will be there with you—as long as you stay connected to Him. Sever that connection, and He'll still be there, of course. You just won't be in a position to access all that He has for you—all the wisdom, all the grace, all the love, all the comfort, all the power to adapt to the changes you're going through. Those who go that route often end up in despair until they find the strength to return to Him, usually after they've hit rock bottom. That's a place where you don't ever want to be.

Stay connected, and you can be assured of having everything you need to make your transition to adulthood a smooth one. With God you can even welcome the changes that will be taking place in your life, because you know that He will not force you to face any situation that you cannot handle. Think of a time recently when you were worried or fearful about a situation in your life. He came through for you then, didn't He? He will continue to come through for you over and over again, as you venture out on your own.

Decide right now that you will continue to rely on God through the coming years. Make an ironclad resolution that regardless of the temptations you'll face to do things your way, you will do things God's way instead. No one knows you better. No one loves you more. No one has your best interests at heart the way He does. No one else can be with you every hour of every day, offering you guidance and strength and safety and answers to your every prayer.

This is it—the moment you've been waiting for. Go ahead; take the plunge. You have the most secure safety net in the world. Your journey of faith is about to get unbelievably exciting. This is not a time for holding back. Go out and get everything that life—or rather, everything that God—has for you. You're going to do just fine.

We are joined together in [Christ's] body by his strong sinews, and we grow only as we get our nourishment and strength from God.
—COLOSSIANS 2:19 NLT

I Will

Realize that change is inevitable. _____ yes _____ no

Face the future with an unshakable confidence in God. _____ yes _____ no

Welcome the changes that the coming years will bring. _____ yes _____ no

Resolve to do things God's way rather than my way. _____ yes _____ no

Stay connected to God in my new environment and
lifestyle. _____ yes _____ no

Understand that God has my best interests at heart. _____ yes _____ no

Realize that God is doing a new thing in my life. _____ yes _____ no

Things to Do

☐ List your fears about the immediate future and give them to God.

☐ Write in your journal about all the reasons you have to be excited
about the future.

☐ Make a list of the things that are about to change in your life. Pray
over each item, asking God for the wisdom and grace to handle each
change.

☐ Ask someone a bit older than you how they handled the toughest
transitions in their life after graduation.

☐ Ask God to bring a strong believer into your life in your new
environment.

☐ Thank God for promising to be with you all the time.

Things to Remember

These tents we now live in are like a heavy burden, and we groan. But we don't do this just because we want to leave these bodies that will die. It is because we want to change them for bodies that will never die.

2 CORINTHIANS 5:4 CEV

[Job said,] "He is unique, and who can make Him change? And whatever His soul desires, that He does."

JOB 23:13 NKJV

Jesus Christ never changes! He is the same yesterday, today, and forever.
Hebrews 13:8 CEV

"I am the LORD, I do not change; therefore you are not consumed, O sons of Jacob."

MALACHI 3:6 NKJV

A little yeast can change a whole batch of dough.

GALATIANS 5:9 CEV

[Heaven and earth] will perish, but You will endure; yes, they will all grow old like a garment; like a cloak You will change them, and they will be changed.

PSALM 102:26 NKJV

Humans give life to their children. Yet only God's Spirit can change you into a child of God.

JOHN 3:6 CEV

[Paul wrote,] I will explain a mystery to you. Not every one of us will die, but we will all be changed. It will happen suddenly, quicker than the blink of an eye. At the sound of the last trumpet the dead will be raised. We will all be changed, so that we will never die again. Our dead and decaying bodies will be changed into bodies that won't die or decay. The bodies we now have are weak and can die. But they will be changed into bodies that are eternal. Then the Scriptures will come true, "Death has lost the battle!"

1 CORINTHIANS 15:51-54 CEV

Change is inevitable. Change for the better is a full-time job.

ADLAI STEVENSON

In a higher world it is otherwise, but here below to live is to change, and to be perfect is to have changed often.

JOHN HENRY NEWMAN

Other books in the Checklist for Life Series

Checklist for Life
ISBN 0-7852-6455-8

Checklist for Life for Teens
ISBN 0-7852-6461-2

Checklist for Life for Women
ISBN 0-7852-6462-0

Checklist for Life for Men
ISBN 0-7852-6463-9